40

DAYS OF
TRANSFORMATION

Cover Design: Cheyanna Rose Pelham

Print ISBN: 979-8-9923412-3-2
Library of Congress Control Number: 2025909365

Pinpoint PUBLISHING
Atlanta, GA
www.Pinpoint.pub

Contents

Dedication

In the last few years, no one has "transformed" more than my lady, my wife, and my best friend of 36 years and counting.

Victoria, I dedicate this book of transformation to you!

You said "YES" to your next!

Foreward

There are people who preach truth, and then there are those who embody it. They live out the gospel in such a way that just being around them awakens something in you. Pastor Manny Rivera is that kind of man.

He is not only my pastor but my spiritual father. His life, his leadership, and his unwavering commitment to walking with boldness have shaped me in ways I'm still discovering. Through both his words and his witness, I've learned that transformation isn't about behavior modification. It's about soul-deep surrender. It's about becoming. And no one teaches that more clearly or models it more authentically than Pastor Manny.

40 Days of Transformation is more than a devotional. It's a roadmap for anyone ready to be changed from the inside out. Day by day, it calls you to reflect deeply, live boldly, and love fully. It invites you into the same kind of process Pastor Manny has walked with humility and courage. It is a process where purpose is discovered, faith is refined, and your life is aligned with God's.

If you're holding this book, I believe it's because God wants to take you on a journey. My encouragement to you is simple: don't rush it. Let each day do its work. Let each truth settle deep. When you finish this journey, you won't just have read Pastor Manny's words. You'll have caught his heart.

And that's where the real transformation begins.

With honor,

Andy McMahon
Executive Pastor, Discover Life Church
Co-founder, Pinpoint Publishing

Introduction to "40 Days of Transformation"

In the hustle and bustle of modern life, we often find ourselves yearning for something deeper—an authentic connection with God that transcends the surface level of routine faith. "40 Days of Transformation" is an invitation to embark on a transformative journey of spiritual growth, where each day brings new insights and challenges to help us become the people God intends us to be.

Spiritual transformation is not merely a change in behavior or habits but a dynamic, holistic process that involves the renewal of the mind, heart, and spirit. It requires an open heart and a willingness to change, allowing God to work from the inside out. This process is beautifully illustrated through the biblical significance of the number 40, which often marks a period of testing and preparation for new beginnings. From Moses' 40 days on Mount Sinai to Jesus' 40 days in the wilderness, these periods of transformation lead to profound spiritual growth and renewal.

The essence of transformation lies in embracing the journey of becoming more like Christ. As the Apostle Paul writes in Romans 12:2, "Do not conform to the pattern of this world, but be transformed by the renewing of your mind." This transformation is about allowing God to reshape our minds and hearts to reflect His love and grace. As you engage with this book, you will be encouraged to look beyond external measures of success and focus on the profound work God is doing within you.

Beginning with the concept of "Buying the Field," you are invited to invest in your spiritual life as you would treasure hidden in a field. This metaphor sets the stage for the journey ahead, where the value of transformation is found in the daily commitment to grow in faith and understanding. It is a call to invest in the eternal, recognizing the priceless nature of a transformed life.

The book offers reflections on key themes such as perseverance in "Don't Quit," highlighting the strength God provides to endure challenges, and the importance of community in "Covenant Community." These chapters remind us that transformation is both an individual and a communal journey, one that thrives in the context of supportive relationships. As believers, we are called to support and encourage one another, recognizing that our growth is intertwined with the community of faith.

Through topics like "Forgiveness, 490 x's... Trust, 1x," you'll explore the liberating power of forgiveness, which is essential for healing and growth. Spiritual transformation involves letting go of past grievances and embracing a future defined by love and grace. Forgiveness is not just an act of release but a profound transformation of the heart that reflects God's mercy and love.

As you read, consider the call to action found in "Christianity is One Big Verb!" This reflection underscores that faith is meant to be lived out actively, challenging you to put your beliefs into practice and make a tangible impact on the world around you. Transformation is not passive; it is an active pursuit of God's will, leading to a life of purpose and impact.

In this book, each day is an opportunity to reflect, learn, and grow. As you journey through these pages, let the insights inspire you to embrace the transformation God offers, leading you to a deeper understanding of His will and purpose for your life. May this book serve as a catalyst for change, encouraging you to seek God's presence in every aspect of your life. As you open your heart to His transformative power, may you experience the profound joy and peace that come from living in alignment with His divine purpose.

The Significance of the Number 40 and Its Prophetic Meaning

Numbers in the Bible often carry profound spiritual and symbolic significance, offering insights into God's character and His plans for humanity. Throughout Scripture, numbers like 21, 40, and 52 appear in key narratives, each with its unique meaning and purpose. The number 21 can symbolize a time of expectation, completion, and perfection, as seen in the 21-day period of Daniel's fasting and prayer (Daniel 10:2-3) that led to divine revelation. The number 40 is frequently associated with periods of testing, trial, and transformation, signifying a time of spiritual preparation and renewal. Meanwhile, the number 52 can symbolize restoration and unity, as demonstrated by Nehemiah's rebuilding of Jerusalem's walls in 52 days (Nehemiah 6:15). These numbers collectively emphasize the importance of God's timing and purpose, guiding us through times of challenge and renewal toward divine fulfillment.

Biblical and Spiritual Insights

In the Bible, the number 40 is often associated with periods of trial and testing that lead to spiritual growth and preparation for new beginnings. Here are some key examples:

1. ***The Flood:*** God caused it to rain for 40 days and 40 nights during the time of Noah (Genesis 7:12). This period was a time of judgment and cleansing for the earth, leading to a new beginning for humanity through Noah's family.

2. **Moses on Mount Sinai:** Moses spent 40 days and nights on Mount Sinai receiving the Law from God (Exodus 24:18). This period of divine revelation and instruction prepared the Israelites for their covenant relationship with God.

3. ***The Israelites' Wilderness Journey:*** The Israelites wandered in the wilderness for 40 years (Numbers 14:33-34). This period was a time of testing and dependence on God, preparing them to enter the Promised Land.

4.   ***Jesus' Temptation:*** Jesus fasted for 40 days and nights in the wilderness, where He was tempted by Satan (Matthew 4:1-2). This period of testing strengthened Him for His public ministry.

5.   ***The Resurrection to Ascension:*** After His resurrection, Jesus appeared to His disciples over 40 days before ascending to heaven (Acts 1:3). This period was a time of instruction and preparation for the disciples to carry out their mission.

Inspirational and Prophetic Application

The number 40 can be seen as a symbol of transformation and preparation, encouraging individuals to embrace periods of testing and growth. Here are some ways the significance of the number 40 can be applied to our lives:

1.   ***Endurance and Perseverance:*** The number 40 reminds us that periods of trial and testing are part of the spiritual journey. Like the Israelites in the wilderness or Jesus in the desert, we are called to endure and persevere through challenging times, trusting in God's provision and strength.

2.   ***Spiritual Preparation:*** Just as Moses and Jesus used their 40-day periods for spiritual preparation, we can use times of trial to deepen our relationship with God and prepare for the next season of life. This may involve prayer, fasting, and seeking God's guidance and wisdom.

3.   ***Renewal and Transformation:*** The number 40 signifies a time of renewal and transformation, where old patterns and behaviors are shed, and new growth occurs. We are invited to embrace change and allow God to transform us from the inside out, leading to greater spiritual maturity and purpose.

4.   ***Trust in God's Timing:*** The 40-day or 40-year periods in the Bible highlight the importance of trusting in God's timing. We are reminded that God is working in our lives, even when the journey seems long and arduous. By

trusting in His plan, we can rest assured that He is leading us toward His intended purpose.

5.   ***Prophetic Vision and Mission:*** Embracing the prophetic meaning of the number 40 encourages us to seek God's vision for our lives. It invites us to align our goals and actions with His divine purpose, stepping into the roles and responsibilities He has prepared for us. By living with intentionality and purpose, we can make a meaningful impact in our world.

The number 40 carries a deep spiritual significance that inspires us to embrace periods of testing, transformation, and renewal. Whether applied to personal growth or communal efforts, it serves as a reminder of God's faithfulness and the transformative power of His grace. As we embark on a 40-day journey of devotion and teaching, let us embrace the prophetic significance of this number, allowing it to guide us into a deeper relationship with God and a more purposeful life.

Day 1

Buying the Field

Matthew 13:44 (NIV) "The kingdom of heaven is like treasure hidden in a field. When a man found it, he hid it again, and then in his joy went and sold all he had and bought that field."

Matthew 19:16-22 (NIV) "16 Just then a man came up to Jesus and asked, 'Teacher, what good thing must I do to get eternal life?' 17 'Why do you ask me about what is good?' Jesus replied. 'There is only One who is good. If you want to enter life, keep the commandments.' 18 'Which ones?' he inquired. Jesus replied, "'You shall not murder, you shall not commit adultery, you shall not steal, you shall not give false testimony, 19 honor your father and mother,' and 'love your neighbor as yourself.' 20 'All these I have kept,' the young man said. 'What do I still lack?' 21 Jesus answered, 'If you want to be perfect, go, sell your possessions and give to the poor, and you will have treasure in heaven. Then come, follow me.' 22 When the young man heard this, he went away sad, because he had great wealth."

Understanding Value and Honor

Proverbs 3:9 (NIV) - "Honor the Lord with your wealth, with the firstfruits of all your crops."

In our lives, the direction we take is often dictated by what we value. Whether we acknowledge it or not, we all practice honor. The truth is that we become the very thing we honor. Honor is more than just recognition of worth or value; it is the commitment to pursue and attain it. Recognizing worth in something or someone is noble, but paying the price to secure it is the true essence of honor.

The Parable of the Hidden Treasure

Philippians 3:7-8 (NIV) - "But whatever were gains to me I now consider loss for the sake of Christ. What is more, I consider everything a loss because of the surpassing worth of knowing Christ Jesus my Lord, for whose sake I have lost all things."

The parable of the hidden treasure in Matthew 13:44 illustrates the journey of a man who discovered something of immeasurable value. This man was in search mode, driven by a desire to find something precious. Pursuit is the prerequisite of recognition, and it's hard to recognize something if you are not actively searching for it. When you seek treasure, you will know it when you see it.

Pursuit and Desire

Desire alone is not enough to accomplish our goals. It is the pursuit that leads to recognition, and recognition allows us to practice honor. The man's desire led him to find the treasure, but finding it was only half the battle. Locating something valuable is one thing; obtaining it is another, and maintaining it is yet a greater task.

A Strategy for Possession

> ***Proverbs 2:4-5 (NIV)*** - "and if you look for it as for silver and search for it as for hidden treasure, then you will understand the fear of the Lord and find the knowledge of God."

To secure his treasure, the man developed a strategy for obtaining it. This required him to sell all he had to buy the field where the treasure was hidden. His actions were bold and extreme, reflecting the nature of true faith in God. Faith is always bold and extreme, demanding that we value God's kingdom above all else.

The Meaning of Desire

> **Psalm 37:4 (NIV)** - "Take delight in the Lord, and he will give you the desires of your heart."

A Biblical understanding of "desire" comes from the Latin roots "De" (from) and "Sire" (Father), meaning "from the Father." True desire, then, is a yearning placed within us by God. It aligns with His purpose and leads us towards His kingdom. When we desire something from God, it motivates us to pursue it wholeheartedly.

Wisdom in Action

James 1:5 (NIV) - "If any of you lacks wisdom, you should ask God, who gives generously to all without finding fault, and it will be given to you."

Just as the man who found the treasure exercised wisdom by purchasing the field, we must also apply wisdom in our pursuit of God's kingdom. He understood that to legally possess the treasure, he needed to own the field. This meant taking responsibility for not only the treasure but everything that came with it.

Practical Application:

- Are you desiring something from the Father?
- Consider the treasure God has placed in your path. What field must you buy to obtain it?

Taking Responsibility for the Whole

Luke 16:10 (NIV) - "Whoever can be trusted with very little can also be trusted with much, and whoever is dishonest with very little will also be dishonest with much."

Many of us desire the contents of the kingdom without taking responsibility for the container. We may want the benefits of a relationship without committing to the stewardship it requires. We desire success without being willing to endure the challenges that come with it. The man in the parable recognized that in order to gain the treasure, he had to buy the entire field.

The Bold Move of Faith

Hebrews 11:6 (NIV) - "And without faith, it is impossible to please God, because anyone who comes to him must believe that he exists and that he rewards those who earnestly seek him."

To buy the field is a bold and extreme move, a reflection of how we should value the purpose of God's kingdom in our lives. Buying the field is not just recognizing worth; it is being willing to pay any price to possess it. Jesus calls us to "buy the field," to invest everything in the pursuit of His kingdom.

Reflection:

- What fields do you need to buy in your life to fully embrace God's kingdom?

- Are you willing to make bold and extreme moves of faith to secure the treasure God has for you?

The Rich Young Ruler

Matthew 6:19-21 (NIV) - "Do not store up for yourselves treasures on earth, where moths and vermin destroy, and where thieves break in and steal. But store up for yourselves treasures in heaven, where moths and vermin do not destroy, and where thieves do not break in and steal. For where your treasure is, there your heart will be also."

The story of the rich young ruler in Matthew 19:16-22 serves as a powerful illustration of this principle. The young man approached Jesus, seeking eternal life, but when challenged to sell all he had and follow Jesus, he walked away sad. Despite recognizing the value of what Jesus offered, he was unwilling to pay the price.

The Challenge of True Honor

The young ruler failed because he honored himself more than what Jesus was offering. He could not see past his wealth to the greater treasure of the kingdom. This is a challenge we all face: will we honor God's kingdom above our own possessions and ambitions?

Will We Buy the Field?

Luke 14:33 (NIV) - "In the same way, those of you who do not give up everything you have cannot be my disciples."

The question remains for us today: Are we willing to buy the field? Are we ready to give up everything we have to obtain all that God has for us? This is not a one-time decision but a daily commitment to pursue God's kingdom with all our heart, soul, and mind.

Practical Steps for Buying the Field:

- *Evaluate Your Priorities:* Reflect on what you value most in your life. Are these aligned with God's kingdom?

- *Commit to Pursuit:* Engage actively in seeking God's will and purpose for your life.

- *Be Willing to Sacrifice:* Identify areas where you need to let go of personal desires to embrace God's plans.

- *Trust God Completely:* Rely on God's guidance and provision as you pursue His kingdom.

Application

In our pursuit of God's kingdom, it's crucial to understand that true value requires sacrifice and commitment. Just like the man who sold everything to buy the field, we are called to prioritize God's kingdom above all else. Begin by evaluating your own priorities and consider what sacrifices you need to make to align your life with God's will. Are there areas in your life where you are holding back from fully committing to God's plans? Reflect on these and take steps towards fully embracing the path God has set before you.

Challenge Questions

1.   What treasure has God placed in your life that requires you to "buy the field" to fully possess it? Reflect on the areas where God is calling you to invest your time, resources, and energy to gain something of greater value.

2.   In what ways do you struggle with prioritizing God's kingdom over your personal desires or ambitions? Identify specific areas where your desires may conflict with God's will and consider how you can align these with His kingdom.

3.   How can you demonstrate bold and extreme faith in your daily life, similar to the man who bought the field? Think about practical steps you can take to show your commitment to God's kingdom, even when it requires personal sacrifice.

As we journey through life, the parable of the hidden treasure reminds us of the value of God's kingdom and the price we must be willing to pay to obtain it. It challenges us to evaluate what we truly honor and whether we are willing to make bold moves of faith to pursue God's purposes.

Day 2

Encouragement

1 Thessalonians 5:14 (NIV) "And we urge you, brothers, warn those who are idle, encourage the timid, help the weak, and be patient with everyone."

The Power of Encouragement

Hebrews 10:24-25 (NIV) - "And let us consider how we may spur one another on toward love and good deeds, not giving up meeting together, as some are in the habit of doing, but encouraging one another—and all the more as you see the Day approaching."

A deficiency in motivation often leads to an inability to pursue our goals and live purposefully. Pursuit is the action of living forcefully, and motivation is the fuel that drives that pursuit. Without motivation, we may find ourselves stagnant and unable to move forward. Encouragement, however, provides the spark needed to ignite motivation. It is, quite literally, the receiving of courage.

In his Epistles, especially those written from prison, the Apostle Paul frequently focused on encouragement. These letters were addressed to his spiritual sons and daughters who were leading the churches he had planted. They were written to encourage those giving their lives for the Gospel's purpose. Paul understood that to motivate his leaders to continue their faith journey, he needed to kindle their motivation with encouragement.

Parakaleo: Calling Alongside

John 14:16 (NIV) - "And I will ask the Father, and he will give you another advocate to help you and be with you forever."

The Greek word for encouragement is parakaleo, which means "to call alongside." This term assumes that its object is under pressure—fearful, weak, or overwhelmed—and it means to strengthen by giving appropriate aid. This is precisely what the Holy Spirit does in our lives daily. He comes alongside us, offering comfort, guidance, and strength.

Encouragement is essential to the believer. It is the medicine of our souls as we stay the course in pursuit of our purpose. It encompasses affirmation, praise, consolation, and exhortation, providing the support we need to persevere.

The Four Pillars of Encouragement

1. Affirmation

Romans 15:5 (NIV) - "May the God who gives endurance and encouragement give you the same attitude of mind toward each other that Christ Jesus had."

Encouragement affirms those who do not see their value and potential. Many of us struggle with feelings of inadequacy and self-doubt, but a word of encouragement can remind us of our worth and the gifts God has placed within us. Affirmation speaks to the heart, reinforcing our identity as beloved children of God.

2. Praise

1 Thessalonians 5:11 (NIV) - "Therefore encourage one another and build each other up, just as in fact you are doing."

Encouragement praises those who are taking scary steps of faith. Walking by faith often involves stepping into the unknown and confronting our fears. Acknowledging the courage of those who take these steps can inspire them to continue and reassure them that they are not alone.

3. Consolation

2 Corinthians 1:4 (NIV) - "Who comforts us in all our troubles, so that we can comfort those in any trouble with the comfort we ourselves receive from God."

Encouragement consoles those who have had their spiritual wind knocked out. Life's challenges and setbacks can leave us feeling defeated and discouraged. In these moments, consolation provides comfort and reassurance, reminding us of God's presence and faithfulness.

4. Exhortation

Hebrews 3:13 (NIV) - "But encourage one another daily, as long as it is called 'Today,' so that none of you may be hardened by sin's deceitfulness."

Encouragement exhorts those who are tempted to give less than their best. We all face moments of fatigue and temptation to settle for less than our best. Exhortation calls us to rise above complacency and pursue excellence in our walk with Christ.

Encouragement in Practice

Galatians 6:2 (NIV) - "Carry each other's burdens, and in this way you will fulfill the law of Christ."

Encouragement is not merely a passive action; it requires intentionality and compassion. Consider how you can practice encouragement in your daily interactions. Look for opportunities to affirm, praise, console, and exhort those around you. Your words of encouragement can make a significant impact on someone's life, providing the motivation they need to persevere.

Practical Application:

• Reflect on someone in your life who may need encouragement. How can you come alongside them and offer support?

• Make it a habit to speak words of affirmation and praise to those around you, recognizing their efforts and potential.

Application

Philippians 4:13 (NIV) - "I can do all this through him who gives me strength."

Encouragement is vital for sustaining motivation and perseverance in our faith journey. It strengthens and uplifts us, enabling us to overcome challenges and continue pursuing our God-given purpose. As believers, we are called to be sources of encouragement for one another, following the example of the Holy Spirit who comes alongside us. By intentionally encouraging those around us, we can help build a community of faith that is resilient, compassionate, and committed to the Gospel.

Challenge Questions

1. **Who in your life needs encouragement right now, and how can you offer them the support they need?** Consider reaching out to someone who may be struggling or feeling overwhelmed and offer them words of affirmation and support.

2. **In what areas of your life do you need encouragement, and how can you seek it from others or God?** Reflect on your own needs for encouragement and be open to receiving it from those around you and through prayer and Scripture.

3. **How can you make encouragement a regular practice in your daily interactions with others?** Think about ways to incorporate encouragement into your routine, making it a natural part of your relationships and community involvement.

Encouragement is a powerful tool that fosters growth, resilience, and community among believers. By choosing to encourage one another, we fulfill a vital role in the body of Christ, strengthening each other for the journey ahead. Let us embrace the call to encourage, knowing that we all need it to pursue our purpose with passion and perseverance. Encourage someone today—because you need it, and so do they.

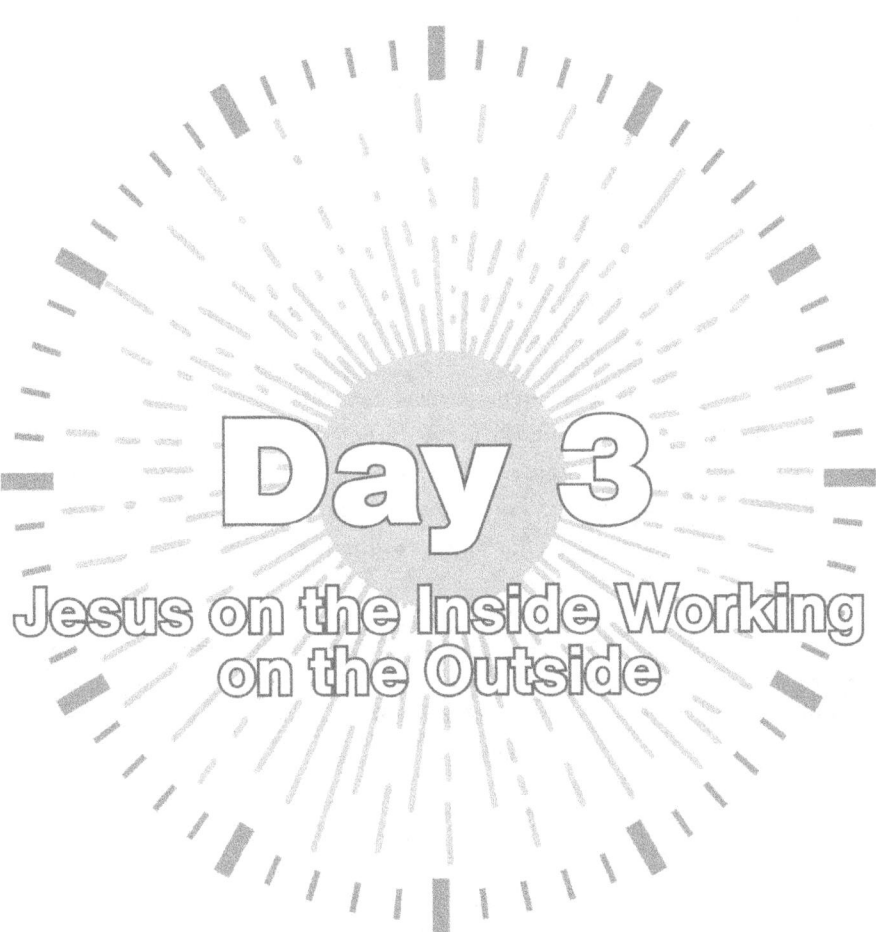

Day 3

Jesus on the Inside Working on the Outside

Ephesians 3:20 (NIV) "Now to Him who is able to do exceedingly abundantly above all that we ask or think, according to the power that works in us…"

The Inside Job

As a new believer, I remember singing the song "Jesus on the Inside Working on the Outside." It captured a profound truth: God is always working within us to transform our surroundings, environment, and future. His work in us is always an "inside job" with the goal of increasing us in every way and making our lives impactful—living BIG and loud with purpose.

God's transformative work begins in the heart, reshaping our thoughts, desires, and actions. This internal transformation inevitably manifests in our external lives, influencing how we interact with the world and fulfill our purpose.

The Power Within

> ***Philippians 2:13 (NIV)*** - "For it is God who works in you to will and to act in order to fulfill his good purpose."

We often focus on what God can do in the "exceedingly abundantly above all that we ask or think." However, the key is in the last part of **Ephesians 3:20:** *"according to the power that works in us."* The word "according" means "depending on whether, or corresponding to the extent to which." This means that God's ability to work through us depends on our willingness to let His power work within us.

The completion of God's work in us was accomplished at Calvary's cross. Now, it's up to us to activate His power in our lives. When we allow His power to continually work in us, it determines God's greatness coming out of us. Our response to His work within us shapes the extent of His work through us.

Embracing Small Beginnings

> ***Zechariah 4:10 (NLT)*** - "Do not despise these small beginnings, for the Lord rejoices to see the work begin…"

If God is processing you through a time of "small beginnings," your season there is determined by your submission to Him as He works in and through you. Your time of "smallness" is meant to cultivate greatness within you. You are not designed to remain small; your humble beginnings are the pathway to greater things.

Small beginnings should not be seen as insignificant. Instead, they are opportunities for growth and preparation. Embrace these seasons with gratitude and anticipation, knowing that God is using them to develop your character and potential.

Cultivating Greatness

Job 8:7 (NIV) - "Though your beginning was small, yet your latter end would increase abundantly."

God's work in us is a process of cultivating greatness. He uses our experiences, challenges, and growth opportunities to shape us into vessels ready to carry out His purposes. The greatness He cultivates within us is not for our glory but for His. As we grow, we reflect His character and love to the world around us.

Cultivating greatness requires patience, perseverance, and trust in God's timing. It involves surrendering our plans and allowing God to shape our lives according to His perfect will.

Application

Reflect on how God is working within you and the areas of your life where you see His transformative power at work. Consider the "small beginnings" in your life and how they are preparing you for greater things. Submit to God's process and allow His power to work within you, trusting that He is faithful to complete the work He has started.

Challenge Questions

1. **What areas of your life reflect God's power working within you?** How can you continue to cultivate these areas? Identify specific aspects of your life where you see God's transformative work and consider how you can further submit to His leading.

2. **How can you embrace the season of small beginnings and trust in God's process for your growth and development?** Reflect on your attitude towards humble beginnings and how you can view them as opportunities for preparation and growth.

3. **In what ways can you allow God's power to work more fully in your life, enabling His greatness to flow through you?** Consider steps you can take to open yourself to God's work within you, such as prayer, study of Scripture, and community involvement.

As we journey through life, let us remember that God's work in us is an "inside job" that transforms us from the inside out. By embracing His process and allowing His power to work within us, we can live lives that reflect His greatness and fulfill our purpose. May we trust in His faithfulness and submit to His leading, knowing that He is working all things together for our good and His glory.

Day 4
Focus with Your Mouth

Matthew 12:36-37 (AMP) : "But I tell you, on the day of judgment, men will have to give account for every idle (inoperative, nonworking) word they speak. For by your words you will be justified and acquitted, and by your words you will be condemned and sentenced."

The Power of Words

> *Proverbs 18:21 (NIV)* - "The tongue has the power of life and death, and those who love it will eat its fruit."

When we hear the word "focus," we immediately think about seeing with the eye or concentrating with the mind. However, there is another way to focus: with our mouths. Jesus places a critical emphasis on this in Matthew 12:36-37. He explains that our words reveal the state of our hearts and have the power to direct our lives.

Our words carry immense power. They do not originate in our mouths but in our hearts, where they are formed. The mouth has a way of discharging what is abundant in the heart. The more words are released, the more the heart creates them. Words portray the direction of your heart—your life's focus!

Words Reveal the Heart

> *Luke 6:45 (NIV)* - "A good man brings good things out of the good stored up in his heart, and an evil man brings evil things out of the evil stored up in his heart. For the mouth speaks what the heart is full of."

Jesus taught that our words are a reflection of our inner state. They are a window into the condition of our hearts. The words we speak reveal our true thoughts, beliefs, and intentions. Therefore, it is crucial to be mindful of what we say, as our words can either build up or tear down, encourage or discourage.

The Consequences of Idle Words

> *Proverbs 12:18 (NIV)* - "The words of the reckless pierce like swords, but the tongue of the wise brings healing."

Jesus warns us about the consequences of idle words. Idle words are those that are inoperative and nonworking—words that are careless and without purpose. A diet of idle words leads to an unhealthy and unproductive life, one without purpose and intention. On the day of judgment, we will be held accountable for every idle word we speak, emphasizing the importance of using our words wisely.

Speaking with Purpose

> ***Ephesians 4:29 (NIV)*** - "Do not let any unwholesome talk come out of your mouths, but only what is helpful for building others up according to their needs, that it may benefit those who listen."

Our focus must be on speaking productive, effective, and purposeful words. Speak what God is speaking to you. Speak out your dreams, your goals, and your promises, for this keeps your focus. When we control our mouths, we are controlling the focus of our lives.

Practical Application:

• Be intentional about the words you speak. Consider if they align with God's truth and purpose for your life.

• Use your words to encourage and build up others, reflecting the love and wisdom of Christ.

Controlling Your Tongue

> **James 3:5-6 (NIV)** - "Likewise, the tongue is a small part of the body, but it makes great boasts. Consider what a great forest is set on fire by a small spark. The tongue also is a fire, a world of evil among the parts of the body. It corrupts the whole body, sets the whole course of one's life on fire, and is itself set on fire by hell."

Controlling our tongues is a crucial aspect of spiritual maturity. The words we speak can have a profound impact on our lives and the lives of others. By focusing on speaking words that align with God's will, we align our lives with His purpose. When we speak life, truth, and encouragement, we create a positive impact and reflect God's love to the world.

Application

Colossians 4:6 (NIV) - "Let your conversation be always full of grace, seasoned with salt, so that you may know how to answer everyone."

Reflect on the words you speak daily and their impact on your life and others. Are your words building up or tearing down? Consider how you can focus your speech to align with God's truth and purpose. Practice speaking words of life and encouragement, and be intentional about using your words to glorify God and bless others.

Challenge Questions

1. **What words are you speaking over your life, and how do they reflect the condition of your heart?** Reflect on the words you use daily and consider what they reveal about your beliefs and attitudes.

2. **How can you use your words to encourage and uplift others, reflecting the love of Christ?** Identify specific ways you can speak life and encouragement to those around you, helping them grow in their faith.

3. **In what ways can you become more intentional about focusing your speech to align with God's purpose for your life?** Consider practical steps you can take to ensure your words are purposeful, effective, and aligned with God's truth.

Words are powerful tools that shape our lives and the lives of those around us. By focusing our speech on what is good, true, and purposeful, we align ourselves with God's will and reflect His character. Let us be mindful of the words we speak, using them to build up, encourage, and guide others in their walk with Christ. In doing so, we will live lives that are impactful, purposeful, and glorifying to God.

Day 5
Don't Quit

Revelation 3:5 (NIV) "He who overcomes will, like them, be dressed in white. I will never blot out his name from the book of life, but will acknowledge his name before my Father and his angels."

The Call to Persevere

James 1:12 (NIV) - "Blessed is the one who perseveres under trial because, having stood the test, that person will receive the crown of life that the Lord has promised to those who love him."

This scripture in Revelation 3:5 has sparked various theological debates, particularly regarding whether we can lose our salvation. While some argue over this, I suggest we conduct ourselves with the mindset that we must remain steadfast in our faith while being secure in the knowledge of God's abundant grace for our mistakes and failures.

Our life in Christ is a series of acts of obedience to directives given by God. This is what purpose is about. Whether you label it as your calling or mission, it is an instruction—an assignment from God that requires less of you and more of Him. It demands faithfulness and the willingness to give your life for His purpose.

Levels of Purpose

Philippians 3:14 (NIV) - "I press on toward the goal to win the prize for which God has called me heavenward in Christ Jesus."

Our purpose is a series of levels. Reaching new levels is only possible by completing what is required at the previous level. Just as graduating from junior high school to senior high school requires proof of finishing the requirements in junior high, this principle applies to every aspect of our natural lives. Promotions in life take us from the top of one level to the bottom of the next. This is where overcoming and endurance take place.

Each level of our purpose brings new challenges and opportunities for growth. God equips us to overcome these challenges as we remain faithful and persevere. The process of moving through these levels strengthens our character and deepens our faith.

Endurance and Overcoming

Hebrews 12:1 (NIV) - "Therefore, since we are surrounded by such a great cloud of witnesses, let us throw off everything that hinders and the sin that so easily entangles. And let us run with perseverance the race marked out for us."

At the heart of our journey is the call to endure and overcome. God has given us the ability to do both. It's as simple as choosing to engage in our purpose and design. This journey will require us to die to ourselves, but even in dying, God provides the grace to do so. We are designed to live and to die—to die to our old selves and live for Christ.

The journey of faith is not always easy, but God promises to be with us every step of the way. He equips us with the strength and perseverance we need to finish the race and fulfill our purpose.

Pressing Forward

2 Timothy 4:7-8 (NIV) - "I have fought the good fight, I have finished the race, I have kept the faith. Now there is in store for me the crown of righteousness, which the Lord, the righteous Judge, will award to me on that day—and not only to me but also to all who have longed for his appearing."

Press forward, overcome to the end, and be whom God intended for you to be. Whatever you do, don't quit! Trust in God's strength and grace to carry you through every challenge and opportunity.

Practical Application:

- Reflect on the areas of your life where you may feel like giving up. Pray for strength and perseverance to continue.

- Encourage others in their journey, reminding them of God's promise to help us endure and overcome.

Application

Galatians 6:9 (NIV) - "Let us not become weary in doing good, for at the proper time we will reap a harvest if we do not give up."

Reflect on your current journey and the levels of purpose you are navigating. Consider how God is calling you to persevere and overcome in these areas. Remember that each challenge is an opportunity to grow and become more like Christ. Commit to pressing forward, knowing that God is with you and will provide the strength you need.

Challenge Questions

1.   **What challenges are you currently facing that require perseverance and endurance?** How can you rely on God's strength to overcome them? Reflect on specific areas where you feel challenged and consider how you can lean on God for strength and guidance.

2.   **How can you encourage others to continue their journey and not quit, even when facing difficulties?** Think about ways to support and uplift those around you, helping them to persevere in their faith journey.

3.   **In what ways can you remind yourself of God's promises to help you endure and overcome?** Identify practical steps you can take to keep God's promises at the forefront of your mind, such as memorizing Scripture or creating a prayer routine.

Perseverance and endurance are vital in our journey of faith. By choosing to press forward and trust in God's strength, we fulfill our purpose and reflect His glory. Let us commit to overcoming every challenge and staying true to our calling, knowing that God is faithful to complete the work He has begun in us. Whatever you do, don't quit! Trust in God's grace and power to carry you through.

Day 6

Did Jesus Ever Get "Me Time?"

Matthew 14:13-14 (NIV) "When Jesus heard what had happened, he withdrew by boat privately to a solitary place. Hearing of this, the crowds followed him on foot from the towns. When Jesus landed and saw a large crowd, he had compassion on them and healed their sick."

The Context of Solitude

Mark 1:35 (NIV) - "Very early in the morning, while it was still dark, Jesus got up, left the house and went off to a solitary place, where he prayed."

What did Jesus hear? What happened? Here's the situation: John the Baptist, Jesus' cousin, was just beheaded. He was the one who baptized Jesus and prepared the way for his ministry. Things were getting crazy and scary in Judea. Martyrs were being created, and Jesus and his disciples were next on the hit list.

We assume Jesus did what was expected of him; he withdrew to chill for a while. We suppose he needed some "me time," considering the circumstances. Have you ever needed some "me time?" There is one thing wrong with "me time" – the name. "Me time" never solves problems. It's a selfish way of not facing issues in life. "Me time" is really supposed to be prayer time.

Jesus's Response to Crisis

Philippians 2:3-4 (NIV) - "Do nothing out of selfish ambition or vain conceit. Rather, in humility value others above yourselves, not looking to your own interests but each of you to the interests of the others."

In Matthew 14:13-14, we see Jesus seeking solitude after the death of John the Baptist. He withdrew to a solitary place, possibly to mourn, pray, and find strength. However, when the crowds followed him, he was moved with compassion and ministered to their needs. Instead of focusing on his own need for solitude, Jesus prioritized the needs of others, demonstrating profound compassion and selflessness.

The neat thing in this passage is that God, the Father, did not allow Jesus to have "me time." On his way to a solitary place, the multitudes followed him. Instead of sending them away, he was moved with compassion and healed them all! He later fed them all as well, over 15,000 in total. Go Jesus!

The Purpose of "Me Time"

Matthew 6:33 (NIV) - "But seek first his kingdom and his righteousness, and all these things will be given to you as well."

"Me time" is often seen as a way to escape the pressures and responsibilities of life. However, true rest and rejuvenation come from aligning ourselves with God's will and seeking His presence. Jesus found strength not in isolation but in communion with the Father and serving others.

Here's my point: most of us would've sent the crowds away. Tough situations in life like tragedies, failures, and deaths are momentum stoppers. They usually halt the forward progression of our calling. Could it be that we were not designed to stop? We cannot bring to a halt the will of God in our lives. When we do, well, it's over. The best way to overcome a crisis is to allow compassion to fill your heart and engage in the will of the Father—touching people and changing lives. It's the best kind of stress reliever—give it a try!

Compassion in Action

Galatians 6:2 (NIV) - "Carry each other's burdens, and in this way you will fulfill the law of Christ."

Jesus's response to the crowds shows us the power of compassion in action. Instead of retreating inward, Jesus engaged with the people, offering healing and hope. His example teaches us that our own healing and fulfillment often come through serving others.

I don't believe in "me time." I knew a lady who called them "mental health days." She could not handle any kind of stress whatsoever and continually needed these "mental health days." In reality, they were dedicated times to become selfishly inward. It's probably why she was never able to engage in God's will and commitment was always a problem. I challenge you today: in tough times of your life, instead of taking "me time," take "people time." Allow compassion to overtake you, touch people, love on them, and minister to them. It'll probably be the best results you will ever have in your ministry.

Application

2 Corinthians 1:3-4 (NIV) - "Praise be to the God and Father of our Lord Jesus Christ, the Father of compassion and the God of all comfort, who comforts us in all our troubles, so that we can comfort those in any trouble with the comfort we ourselves receive from God."

Reflect on your current approach to rest and solitude. Are you seeking "me time" as an escape, or are you aligning your time with God's purpose? Consider how you can use your time to seek God's presence, serve others, and find true rest in Him.

Challenge Questions

1. **How can you transform your "me time" into meaningful time with God that strengthens your faith and equips you to serve others?** Reflect on how you can prioritize prayer and communion with God during your times of rest.

2. **In what ways can you practice compassion in action, following Jesus's example of prioritizing others' needs over your own?** Identify opportunities to serve and minister to others, especially when you feel overwhelmed or stressed.

3. **How can you cultivate a lifestyle that balances rest and service, ensuring you are both spiritually nourished and actively engaged in God's work?** Consider practical steps you can take to maintain a healthy balance between rest and ministry.

Jesus's life teaches us the power of compassion and service, even in times of personal need. By prioritizing others and seeking God's presence, we find true rest and fulfillment. Let us follow His example, transforming our "me time" into opportunities to connect with God and serve others, bringing healing and hope to a world in need.

Day 7

Who Cut in on You?

Galatians 5:7 (NIV) "You were running a good race. Who cut in on you and kept you from obeying the truth?"

The Race of Faith

Hebrews 12:1-2 (NIV) - "Therefore, since we are surrounded by such a great cloud of witnesses, let us throw off everything that hinders and the sin that so easily entangles. And let us run with perseverance the race marked out for us, fixing our eyes on Jesus, the pioneer and perfecter of faith."

In the race of faith, we are called to run with perseverance and focus. Distractions and obstacles can easily cut in on us, hindering our progress and keeping us from obeying the truth. Like the believers in Galatia, we must be vigilant and guard our hearts against anything that might disrupt our connection with God.

Recognizing Distractions

1 Peter 5:8 (NIV) - "Be alert and of sober mind. Your enemy the devil prowls around like a roaring lion looking for someone to devour."

In the days when blogging was more popular than it is today, there was a day I was unable to meet my deadline to post my blog for my email subscribers. The blogs had to be posted before 11:00 a.m. EST for them to go out that day. My routine was as usual. I'm up around 7:30 a.m. every day, regardless of how late I had to stay up the night before. I do my reading, praying, and writing in the first three hours of the day. My routine was flawless until something happened...

I was just about finished with my blog when I realized I was no longer connected to the Internet. It was odd; I hadn't had much trouble with our internet service. I did what I was trained to do by my I.T. guys at the office; I checked all my connections and reset the modem and router, but still nothing. So I called my company. The rep, reading through Q-cards, had me run through the exact steps as before (bless her heart!). Needless to say, it was very frustrating, and yes, I missed my deadline.

While sitting in my office sulking, I heard the deep sound of a diesel engine. I'd heard it before; it sounded like the sound of a drill. It was coming from down the street. I wondered if one of the neighbors was digging a well. I live in the Ranches; people do that kind of stuff around here. I put some shoes on and went on my journey down the street, following the noise. Yes, I was right (so proud of myself); it was exactly that! The drill truck cut the cable line! They apologized, but the damage was done. There I stood, holding the cable line in my hand, wishing I could somehow put it together. My world was crashing in all around me; not only could I not post my blog, but I was disconnected from the world! Well, the cable guys showed up nine hours later. And behold, I am connected to the world again!

Maintaining Your Connection

John 15:5 (NIV) - "I am the vine; you are the branches. If you remain in me and I in you, you will bear much fruit; apart from me you can do nothing."

What's my point? I learned that at any given moment in time, I could lose my connection and stop my momentum. Anything has the power to cut in on you. Anything has the power to be a distraction and a routine breaker. Be careful out there—be mindful of what you allow into your yard (mind and heart), and keep your connection to the Lord holy. Set it apart, honor it, and give it value. Guard your heart, ears, and affections. Don't let anyone or anything cut in on you and keep you from obeying the Lord. Keep your time with Him. It has to be non-negotiable.

Guarding Your Heart

Proverbs 4:23 (NIV) - "Above all else, guard your heart, for everything you do flows from it."

Guarding your heart means being intentional about what you allow into your life. It involves setting boundaries and prioritizing your relationship with God. This requires discipline and vigilance, ensuring that distractions do not cut in on your race of faith.

Practical Application:

- Evaluate the distractions in your life and consider how they may be affecting your relationship with God.

- Establish a daily routine that prioritizes time with God, making it a non-negotiable part of your day.

Application

Philippians 4:8 (NIV) - "Finally, brothers and sisters, whatever is true, whatever is noble, whatever is right, whatever is pure, whatever is lovely, whatever is admirable—if anything is excellent or praiseworthy—think about such things."

Reflect on your current race of faith and the obstacles that may be cutting in on you. Consider how you can refocus your attention on God and maintain a strong connection with Him. Guard your heart and mind against distractions, and commit to running the race with perseverance and purpose.

Challenge Questions

1. **What are the main distractions in your life that cut in on your spiritual journey, and how can you address them?** Reflect on specific areas where distractions hinder your focus on God, and consider practical steps to eliminate or manage them.

2. **How can you establish a routine that prioritizes your relationship with God and guards your time with Him?** Identify ways to create a daily schedule that includes dedicated time for prayer, Bible study, and worship.

3. **In what ways can you stay connected to God even when facing unexpected disruptions or challenges?** Consider strategies for maintaining your spiritual connection, such as Scripture memorization or creating a peaceful prayer space.

In the race of faith, maintaining our connection with God is vital. By guarding our hearts and prioritizing our relationship with Him, we can overcome distractions and stay focused on His truth. Let us run the race with perseverance, keeping our eyes fixed on Jesus, and trusting Him to guide us through every challenge and distraction.

Day 8

Instant...Bam!

Philippians 1:6 (NIV) "Being confident of this, that he who began a good work in you will carry it on to completion until the day of Christ Jesus."

The Process of God's Kingdom

> ***Ecclesiastes 3:11 (NIV)*** - "He has made everything beautiful in its time. He has also set eternity in the human heart; yet no one can fathom what God has done from beginning to end."

There is nothing instant about the Kingdom of God. Many of you have probably already noticed that God works in your life through processes and time. He who began a good work in you will be faithful to complete it. His work in us is complete when we die or when God cracks open the eastern skies and returns with His angels. In other words, there is no such thing as instant maturity, instant understanding, or instant power. We are His workmanship, His poiema in the Greek, meaning His work of art. We are meticulously and unhurriedly processed and put together like an artist paints his picture, or like a master chef prepares a dish—not like we quickly nuke stuff up in a microwave.

The Value of Instant Obedience

> **Isaiah 30:21 (NIV)** - "Whether you turn to the right or to the left, your ears will hear a voice behind you, saying, 'This is the way; walk in it.'"

But I have discovered that instant is not all that bad. God might not respond to us or work in us instantly, but we must reciprocate instantly. In other words, God's work in us might not be instant, but our work for God has to be instant. I was reminded yesterday about instant obedience.

Instant obedience is an immediate response to the voice of God. He speaks to our hearts softly, in a still small voice, but we must respond instantly and immediately. He convicts us about certain issues in our lives so we can respond instantly, knowing very well that every waking second that passes by without obeying is disobedience. Disobedience is the very thing that separates us from the will, plan, purpose, and process of God. It hinders the artist from finishing His masterpiece.

Redeeming the Time

Ephesians 5:15-17 (NIV) - "Be very careful, then, how you live—not as unwise but as wise, making the most of every opportunity, because the days are evil. Therefore do not be foolish, but understand what the Lord's will is."

The currency of the Kingdom of God is time. We are given a certain amount of time in life to fulfill the will of God. In our disobedience, we must embrace the grace of God and be very careful how we live. We must live wisely, redeeming the time, because the days are evil. This is only accomplished through instant obedience. The term "instant" refers to time that has to be redeemed. Simply put, it means making the most of every opportunity the Lord gives us to obey Him.

The Call to Immediate Action

James 1:22 (NIV) - "Do not merely listen to the word, and so deceive yourselves. Do what it says."

Instant obedience requires us to act immediately upon God's guidance and instruction. It involves trusting His wisdom and responding with a willing heart. Delayed obedience is disobedience, and it can hinder the fulfillment of God's purposes in our lives.

Practical Application:

• Reflect on the areas where God is calling you to act immediately. Consider what steps you need to take to respond with instant obedience.

• Pray for sensitivity to God's voice and the courage to act promptly when He speaks.

Application

Colossians 3:23-24 (NIV) - "Whatever you do, work at it with all
your heart, as working for the Lord, not for human masters, since you
know that you will receive an inheritance from the Lord as a reward. It is
the Lord Christ you are serving."

Reflect on how you can practice instant obedience in your daily life. Consider
the areas where you may have delayed in responding to God's voice, and commit to acting promptly and faithfully. Trust that God's timing is perfect, and
embrace the opportunities He gives you to fulfill His will.

Challenge Questions

1.   **In what areas of your life have you delayed obedience to God's instructions, and how can you take immediate action to align with His will?** Reflect on specific areas where you may have hesitated to obey God and consider practical steps to respond promptly.

2.   **How can you cultivate a heart that is sensitive to God's voice and willing to act instantly upon His guidance?** Identify ways to strengthen your spiritual sensitivity, such as prayer, meditation, and study of Scripture.

3.   **What opportunities has God given you to make the most of your time and fulfill His purposes, and how can you seize them with urgency?** Consider the opportunities in your life where God is calling you to act and how you can prioritize His work with immediate obedience.

Instant obedience is a vital part of our faith journey, enabling us to respond to God's call and fulfill His purposes. By making the most of every opportunity and acting promptly, we align ourselves with His will and become active participants in His Kingdom. Let us pray for the wisdom and courage to respond instantly to God's voice, trusting that His timing and plans are perfect.

Day 9
Take the Shot!

James 4:17 (NIV) "Anyone, then, who knows the good he ought to do and doesn't do it, sins."

Managing Life's Greatest Commodity

Ephesians 5:15-16 (NIV) - "Be very careful, then, how you live—not as unwise but as wise, making the most of every opportunity, because the days are evil."

Life is about management. The greatest commodity we manage in life is time. When others are wasting time, successful people are getting ahead. Time is precious, and how we use it determines our impact and success.

When life becomes complicated with issues, we tend to hesitate in all we do or desire to become. Hesitation is detrimental to forward progress. There are many reasons why people hesitate, but it is often rooted in fear. The definition of "hesitate" is to be slow to act—to pause while doing or saying something, often because of uncertainty or doubt.

The Danger of Hesitation

Proverbs 29:25 (NIV) - "Fear of man will prove to be a snare, but whoever trusts in the Lord is kept safe."

In war, soldiers are trained to never hesitate. Hesitation can place their lives in danger and, worse yet, those with them and around them. Movement is always vital! Fear will always paralyze. When fear in war paralyzes you, well—you die.

Indecision causes you to waste time. Never be an archer who looks at a target and says, "ready aim, aim, aim, aim, aim…" Most people are great aimers. They boast about their aiming. They teach classes on aiming. They go to conferences on aiming. They might even have an aiming ministry! The truth is that aiming is only your potential. Taking the shot is your purpose.

From Potential to Purpose

Philippians 3:13-14 (NIV) - "Brothers and sisters, I do not consider myself yet to have taken hold of it. But one thing I do: Forgetting what is behind and straining toward what is ahead, I press on toward the goal to win the prize for which God has called me heavenward in Christ Jesus."

People who always hesitate will always worship their potential. They are satisfied with just aiming. They know what they should do but never get around to doing it.

In James 4:17, the apostle says, "…anyone, then, who knows the good he ought to do and doesn't do it, sins."

Aiming and never shooting is simply sin. The word "sin" (**hamartia**) means to "miss the mark, as an archer shooting at a target." Aiming and never shooting is missing the mark. I would rather shoot and miss than aim and not take the shot. Never hesitate.

Taking the Shot

Colossians 3:23-24 (NIV) - "Whatever you do, work at it with all your heart, as working for the Lord, not for human masters, since you know that you will receive an inheritance from the Lord as a reward. It is the Lord Christ you are serving."

Taking the shot requires courage and trust in God's guidance. It involves moving beyond fear and uncertainty and stepping into action. God calls us to be doers of His Word, not just hearers. By taking the shot, we fulfill our purpose and make the most of the opportunities God gives us.

Practical Application:

• Identify areas where you may be hesitating to take action. Consider what steps you can take to move forward with confidence and faith.

• Reflect on the potential opportunities God has placed before you and how you can act on them.

Application

Joshua 1:9 (NIV) - "Have I not commanded you? Be strong and courageous. Do not be afraid; do not be discouraged, for the Lord your God will be with you wherever you go."

Reflect on your current approach to decision-making and action. Are you hesitating or failing to take the shot? Consider how you can embrace courage and trust God's leading to move from potential to purpose. Commit to taking the shot and making the most of every opportunity to serve and glorify God.

Challenge Questions

1.   **What areas of your life are you hesitating to take action on, and how can you overcome the fear and uncertainty holding you back?** Reflect on specific situations where hesitation has hindered your progress, and consider steps to move forward with confidence.

2.   **How can you shift your focus from aiming to taking the shot, ensuring you act on your potential and fulfill your purpose?** Identify practical ways to transition from preparation to action, embracing opportunities God provides.

3.   **In what ways can you trust God's guidance as you take action and step into your purpose with confidence and courage?** Consider how you can rely on God's promises and presence to guide you as you take bold steps in faith.

In the race of life, hesitation can hinder our progress and prevent us from fulfilling our purpose. By taking the shot and trusting in God's guidance, we can move from potential to purpose and make a meaningful impact for His Kingdom. Let us embrace courage and confidence, knowing that God is with us and will guide us in every step we take.

Day 10
Forgiveness, 490 x's... Trust, 1x

Matthew 18:21-22 (NIV) "Then Peter came to Him and said, 'Lord, how often shall my brother sin against me, and I forgive him? Up to seven times?' Jesus said to him, 'I do not say to you, up to seven times, but up to seventy times seven.'"

The Radical Call to Forgive

Ephesians 4:31-32 (NIV) - "Get rid of all bitterness, rage and anger, brawling and slander, along with every form of malice. Be kind and compassionate to one another, forgiving each other, just as in Christ God forgave you."

490 times. That is how many times Jesus says for us to forgive someone who undeniably, indisputably, purposefully, and with determination sinned against us. Wow, is that even possible for someone to undeniably, indisputably, purposefully, and with determination personally sin against us 490 times? I would think, first time, shame on them; second time, shame on me... I guess I'm wired differently.

Jesus has a way of always blowing our minds. For almost three years, Jesus has been confronting, stretching, and challenging the paradigms of the disciples, preparing them to lead and continue the work of the kingdom of God. So Peter, who answered correctly earlier when he declared Jesus to be the Messiah, decided to ask and answer his own question. He asked, "Lord, how often shall my brother sin against me, and I forgive him? Up to seven times?" Peter assumed he should go overboard and more than double what the law and the prophets required. They required only three times. Peter thought he was going over and above, the extra mile; he thought his answer was sufficient. Jesus, once again, blew him away. He said 70 x 7, 490 times!

The Heart of Forgiveness

Colossians 3:13 (NIV) - "Bear with each other and forgive one another if any of you has a grievance against someone. Forgive as the Lord forgave you."

There is nothing mystical and revelatory about the numbers themselves. Jesus used a hyperbole. His intention was to teach that there are no set legal amounts to forgive. His objective was to teach that unforgiveness could never be justified.

Let's get real here... if you allow someone to purposefully hurt and offend you 490 times in your lifetime, you have issues. There is nothing wrong with removing people from your life. In other words, quit hanging with people who purposefully desire to hurt you.

The truth is that you are Biblically required to forgive and love people who decisively sin and offend you; but you are not Biblically required to trust them. Forgiveness must be given, but trust must be earned.

Distinguishing Forgiveness from Trust

Proverbs 4:23 (NIV) - "Above all else, guard your heart, for everything you do flows from it."

Forgiveness and trust are distinct concepts. While forgiveness is a command that reflects God's grace and mercy toward us, trust must be built over time and through consistent behavior. Forgiving someone does not mean allowing them to continue hurting us. We are called to forgive freely, but trust requires discernment and boundaries.

I have no problem forgiving people. I have much to be forgiven of; therefore, I am a very forgiving person. But, I also have no problem displacing people from my life that I don't trust anymore. When I say displacing people, I mean not allowing them to be integrated in my heart with people who have won over my trust. This protects my heart from being injured and contaminated with unforgiveness. What I do is file people in a place in my life where I don't have to trust them anymore; I don't have to worry about them purposefully sinning against me anymore. I forgave them. That time shame on them, next time shame on me... I know this might bring up questions, so let me hear them...

The Balance of Forgiveness and Boundaries

Romans 12:18 (NIV) - "If it is possible, as far as it depends on you, live at peace with everyone."

Forgiveness involves releasing bitterness and resentment, allowing us to heal and move forward. It reflects Christ's love and sets us free from the burden of holding onto past hurts. However, maintaining healthy boundaries is essential to protect ourselves and ensure that we are not continually hurt by those who have wronged us.

Practical Application:

• Reflect on relationships where forgiveness is needed. Consider how you can forgive while also establishing appropriate boundaries.

• Pray for wisdom and discernment to navigate the balance between forgiveness and trust.

Application

Matthew 6:14-15 (NIV) - "For if you forgive other people when they sin against you, your heavenly Father will also forgive you. But if you do not forgive others their sins, your Father will not forgive your sins."

Reflect on the areas where forgiveness and trust intersect in your life. Consider how you can extend forgiveness to those who have wronged you while wisely determining whether trust can be rebuilt. Seek God's guidance and strength as you navigate these relationships, and commit to living in grace and truth.

Challenge Questions

1.   **What relationships in your life require for-giveness, and how can you extend grace to those who have wronged you?** Reflect on specific instances where forgiveness is needed, and consider how you can take steps to release bitterness and embrace healing.

2.   **How can you establish healthy boundaries with those who have broken your trust, ensuring you protect your heart while maintaining a spirit of forgiveness?** Identify practical ways to set boundaries that safeguard your emotional and spiritual well-being.

3.   **In what ways can you seek God's guidance in balancing forgiveness with discernment, trusting Him to lead you in your interactions with oth-ers?** Consider how prayer and Scripture can guide you in making wise decisions about forgiveness and trust.

Forgiveness is a foundational aspect of our faith, reflecting God's love and grace toward us. While we are called to forgive generously, we must also exercise discernment in whom we trust. By embracing forgiveness and establishing healthy boundaries, we can experience freedom and peace in our relationships. Let us seek God's wisdom as we navigate the complexities of forgiveness and trust, trusting Him to guide us in all our interactions.

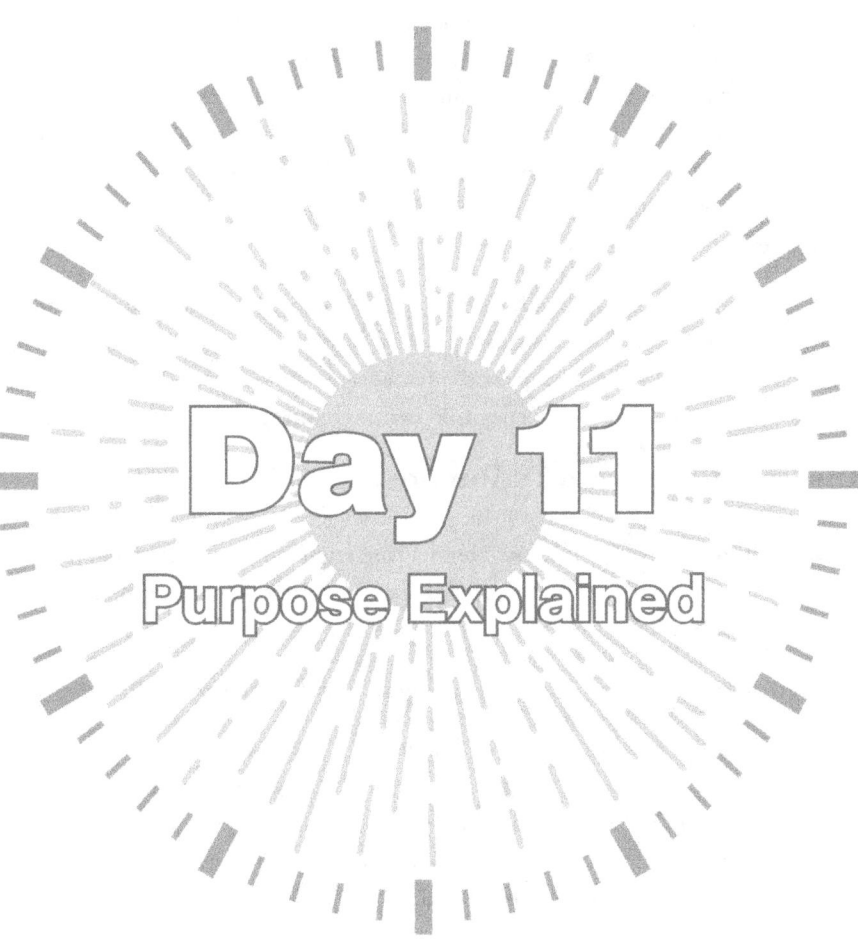

Day 11
Purpose Explained

Proverbs 19:21 (NIV) "Many are the plans in a person's heart, but it is the Lord's purpose that prevails."

Breaking the Cycle of Existence

Ephesians 2:10 (NIV) - "For we are God's handiwork, created in Christ Jesus to do good works, which God prepared in advance for us to do."

The cycles of just existing continue on a daily basis. People live their lives without goals or directives. Millions upon millions of people wake up, get dressed, go to work, come home, eat dinner, and watch television, and go to sleep. This cycle continues in the lives of people who are just surviving. Every day is lived like this without questioning the insanity of it. The truth of the matter is that most people are living their lives by accident, reacting to its outcomes, but never living their lives on purpose.

When we discover how to live life on purpose, our lives do not become redundant, but abundant—abundant in the resources that come with living a life of realized purpose. Living with purpose transforms our existence from a monotonous routine into a vibrant journey filled with meaning and direction.

Understanding God's Purpose

Isaiah 46:10 (NIV) - "I make known the end from the beginning, from ancient times, what is still to come. I say, 'My purpose will stand, and I will do all that I please.'"

Here are four key points concerning purpose. Ponder them:

1. **God is a God of Purpose.** Everything God does is intentional and purposeful. He is not random or chaotic but deliberate in His plans and actions. Understanding that God is a God of purpose helps us trust that our lives have meaning and direction in His greater plan.

2. **Everything Created by God has a Purpose.** *Romans 8:28 (NIV)* - "And we know that in all things God works for the good of those who love him, who have been called according to his purpose." Every creation, from the smallest creature to the vast universe, has a purpose ordained by God.

74

We, too, are created with a specific purpose, uniquely designed to fulfill His plan. Recognizing that we are part of God's design encourages us to seek our role in His creation.

3.   *Not Every Purpose is Understood. Jeremiah 29:11 (NIV)* - "For I know the plans I have for you," declares the Lord, "plans to prosper you and not to harm you, plans to give you hope and a future." While God has a purpose for everything, we may not always understand it. Sometimes, His plans are beyond our comprehension, requiring us to trust in His wisdom and timing. Embracing the mystery of God's purpose challenges us to have faith and rely on His guidance.

4.   *Abuse is Certain Whenever Purpose is Misunderstood. Proverbs 3:5-6 (NIV)* - "Trust in the Lord with all your heart and lean not on your own understanding; in all your ways submit to him, and he will make your paths straight." When we misunderstand or ignore our purpose, we risk misusing our gifts and potential. Abuse occurs when we deviate from God's design, leading to unfulfillment and confusion. Understanding our purpose helps us live in alignment with God's intentions, avoiding the pitfalls of misuse.

Living with Purpose

Philippians 3:13-14 (NIV) - "Brothers and sisters, I do not consider myself yet to have taken hold of it. But one thing I do: Forgetting what is behind and straining toward what is ahead, I press on toward the goal to win the prize for which God has called me heavenward in Christ Jesus."

Living with purpose involves seeking God's will and aligning our lives with His plans. It means actively pursuing the goals and tasks He sets before us, trusting that He will guide us every step of the way. As we live purposefully, we find fulfillment and joy in knowing we are part of God's greater story.

Practical Application:

- Reflect on your current life and identify areas where you may be living by accident rather than on purpose. Consider how you can align your actions with God's purpose for you.

- Seek God's guidance through prayer and Scripture, asking Him to reveal His purpose and direction for your life.

-

Application

Psalm 139:16 (NIV) - "Your eyes saw my unformed body; all the days ordained for me were written in your book before one of them came to be."

Reflect on how you can embrace God's purpose in your life, seeking to understand and live according to His design. Consider how you can break free from the cycle of mere existence and pursue a life of abundance and purpose. Trust in God's plans, knowing that He has created you with intention and for a reason.

Challenge Questions

1.   **How can you discover and embrace the specific purpose God has for your life, ensuring you live with intentionality and direction?** Reflect on your gifts, passions, and opportunities, and consider how they align with God's purpose for you.

2.   **What steps can you take to break free from the cycle of existence and pursue a life of purpose and abundance in Christ?** Identify practical actions you can take to shift from surviving to thriving, seeking God's guidance in your journey.

3.   **In what ways can you trust God's purpose even when you do not fully understand His plans, relying on His wisdom and guidance?** Consider how you can cultivate faith and patience as you navigate the uncertainties of life, trusting in God's perfect timing.

Living with purpose transforms our lives from a cycle of existence to a journey of abundance and meaning. By seeking God's will and understanding our role in His plan, we find fulfillment and joy in our daily walk. Let us embrace the purpose for which we were created, trusting in God's wisdom and guidance as we live intentionally for His glory.

Day 12

Boredom

2 Samuel 11:1 (NIV) "In the spring, at the time when kings go off to war, David sent Joab out with the king's men and the whole Israelite army. They destroyed the Ammonites and besieged Rabbah. But David remained in Jerusalem."

Boredom and Faith

Hebrews 11:1 (NIV) - "Now faith is confidence in what we hope for and assurance about what we do not see."

I don't understand boredom. I can't comprehend how a Christian can actually be bored. I believe that boredom is just flat-out wrong. Boredom and faith—the two are opposites of each other. In other words, I believe when you are bored it means that you are living a lifestyle completely opposite of how the Bible says you are supposed to live. Think about it…if you are supposed to live a life of faith, how can that ever be boring? Can "faith" actually be faith in an attitude of boredom? Impossible!

Faith is meant to be dynamic and active, filled with purpose and direction. When we live by faith, we embrace the unknown and step into God's plans with excitement and anticipation. A life of faith is never stagnant but continually growing and evolving as we seek God's guidance and pursue His purpose.

The Dangers of Boredom

James 1:14-15 (NIV) - "But each person is tempted when they are dragged away by their own evil desire and enticed. Then, after desire has conceived, it gives birth to sin; and sin, when it is full-grown, gives birth to death."

The Danish philosopher and theologian Soren Kierkegaard believed that boredom is the root of all evil. Meaning, that from the state of boredom, the acts of sin and evil originate and are carried out. It's what happened to King David. He was supposed to be at war, doing what God anointed him to do; instead, he stayed home and became bored. One evening, he went for a walk on the roof of his palace and saw Bathsheba (I've always wondered if they called her that because she was taking a "bath" when David saw her? Hmm…) Anyways… And the rest was history…

When we, as Christians, become bored, it is because we have already committed the sin of omission. We have allowed idols to overtake our hearts and have become indifferent to the passion of Christ. Our lives became too easy, too predictable, and too comfortable. We lost our sense of adventure.

Rediscovering Purpose and Passion

Colossians 3:23 (NIV) - "Whatever you do, work at it with all your heart, as working for the Lord, not for human masters."

Let's examine our hearts... Let's not be bored with the message and mission of the Gospel. How can we be bored with helping, touching, and serving people? Let's not be evil people; rather, let's be people of passion and responsibility.

Living with purpose involves actively engaging in the work God has set before us. It requires us to move beyond comfort and predictability and embrace the adventure of following Christ. By reigniting our passion for the Gospel, we can overcome boredom and live lives that are vibrant and impactful.

Embracing the Adventure of Faith

2 Timothy 1:7 (NIV) - "For the Spirit God gave us does not make us timid, but gives us power, love and self-discipline."

Faith invites us into a life of adventure and discovery. It challenges us to step out of our comfort zones and trust God with our future. As we embrace the adventure of faith, we find fulfillment and joy in serving God and others, knowing that our lives have eternal significance.

Practical Application:

- Reflect on areas of your life where you may be experiencing boredom or complacency. Consider how you can reignite your passion and purpose.

- Seek opportunities to serve others and engage in the work of the Gospel, allowing God to use you to make a difference.

Application

1 Corinthians 15:58 (NIV) - "Therefore, my dear brothers and sisters, stand firm. Let nothing move you. Always give yourselves fully to the work of the Lord, because you know that your labor in the Lord is not in vain."

Reflect on how you can live a life of purpose and adventure, embracing the opportunities God provides to serve and impact others. Consider how you can overcome boredom by aligning your life with God's mission and allowing His Spirit to guide you in every endeavor.

Challenge Questions

1.   **In what areas of your life do you feel bored or complacent, and how can you actively seek to reignite your passion for God's purpose?** Reflect on specific situations where boredom has taken root and consider steps to rediscover your passion and commitment to God's work.

2.   **How can you embrace the adventure of faith, stepping out of your comfort zone and trusting God to lead you into new opportunities for growth and service?** Identify practical ways to pursue God's calling with excitement and courage, even when it requires change and risk.

3.   **What steps can you take to align your life with God's mission, ensuring that your time and energy are dedicated to His Kingdom work?** Consider how you can prioritize your relationship with God and seek His guidance in every area of your life, making His mission your own.

Boredom has no place in a life of faith. By embracing the adventure and purpose God has set before us, we can overcome complacency and live vibrant lives filled with meaning and direction. Let us seek to serve God and others passionately, trusting Him to guide us in every step of our journey.

Day 13
Intentional Blindness

Psalm 51:10-12 (NIV) "Create in me a pure heart, O God, and renew a steadfast spirit within me. Do not cast me from your presence or take your Holy Spirit from me. Restore to me the joy of your salvation and grant me a willing spirit, to sustain me."

The Trap of Routine and Familiarity

> **Revelation 2:4-5 (NIV)** - "Yet I hold this against you: You have for-saken the love you had at first. Consider how far you have fallen! Repent and do the things you did at first."

I have read and prayed this Psalm many times. I've especially prayed with sincerity the 12th verse: "Restore to me the joy of your salvation and grant me a willing spirit, to sustain me." Something happened to David that made him lose the joy and passion of his relationship with God. He became bored and committed adultery, murder, lied, coveted, etc. All of us are susceptible to this. It is within the human psyche that we become familiar and fall into the trap of routine. We must be very careful.

This phenomenon is common in many aspects of life. We tend to call it "the honeymoon is over." Enter the bride and groom. They have the joy and expec-tation of getting married, coupled with romance, vacation, and going to an ex-citing place to play and relax. Many never make it past three months after the honeymoon. Successful marriages remain successful by staying away from the trap of routine and familiarity. Likewise, the birth of their first child is absolute-ly thrilling and amazing until the diapers, feedings, and sleepless nights arrive. Again, there is a key to keeping the joy and removing the trap of routine.

Understanding Intentional Blindness

> **2 Corinthians 4:18 (NIV)** - "So we fix our eyes not on what is seen, but on what is unseen, since what is seen is temporary, but what is unseen is eternal."

Psychologists call this intentional blindness. It is also known as perceptual blindness. This is the phenomenon of not being able to see things that are actu-ally there. We lose our internal frame of reference to perceive the importance and value of things we once held in significance. This is due to how our minds see and process information. In other words, we lose focus and sight of things once thought of as beautiful and valuable by allowing our affections to be di-rected toward our lusts. What happens next is that the sacred becomes routine. We begin to forfeit spiritual adventure and lose the joy of our salvation.

Restoring Joy and Spiritual Adventure

Ephesians 1:18 (NIV) - "I pray that the eyes of your heart may be enlightened in order that you may know the hope to which he has called you, the riches of his glorious inheritance in his holy people."

Where is the hope? Glad you asked. Enter the Holy Spirit. We don't have to sin miserably and then repent, like King David, in order for the intentional blindness to be removed. That is way too risky. Many are never restored. We must now seek and pursue the Lord, even if we are having a difficult time seeing the promises. Allow the Holy Spirit to be your counselor and ask Him to convict you and comfort you. Ask Him to direct you away from routine and to help keep your relationship with Him fresh! Pray that the "eyes of your heart may be enlightened in order that you may know the hope to which He has called you, the riches of His glorious inheritance in the saints..." (Ephesians 1:18)

The Holy Spirit empowers us to see beyond the mundane and rediscover the beauty and significance of our relationship with God. By relying on His guidance and presence, we can maintain a vibrant and dynamic faith.

Keeping the Relationship Fresh

John 14:26 (NIV) - "But the Advocate, the Holy Spirit, whom the Father will send in my name, will teach you all things and will remind you of everything I have said to you."

To keep our relationship with God fresh, we must intentionally pursue Him and seek His presence. This involves dedicating time for prayer, worship, and meditation on His Word. It requires a willingness to step out of our comfort zones and embrace the adventure of faith. By doing so, we allow the Holy Spirit to continually renew and refresh our spirits.

Practical Application:

- Reflect on areas of your life where you may have lost sight of God's promises or become trapped in routine. Consider how you can refocus your heart and mind on His eternal purposes.

- Seek the Holy Spirit's guidance in prayer, asking Him to renew your passion and joy for God's presence and mission.

Application

Romans 12:2 (NIV) - "Do not conform to the pattern of this world, but be transformed by the renewing of your mind. Then you will be able to test and approve what God's will is—his good, pleasing and perfect will."

Reflect on how you can overcome intentional blindness and maintain a vibrant relationship with God. Consider how you can embrace the Holy Spirit's work in your life, allowing Him to guide you away from routine and into a dynamic and fulfilling faith journey.

Challenge Questions

1.   **In what areas of your spiritual life have you become trapped in routine, and how can you renew your passion and joy for God's presence?** Reflect on specific practices or attitudes that may have led to complacency, and consider steps to revitalize your relationship with God.

2.   **How can you invite the Holy Spirit to guide you away from intentional blindness and into a deeper understanding of God's promises and purposes?** Identify ways to cultivate a greater awareness of the Holy Spirit's presence and allow Him to illuminate your heart and mind.

3.   **What practical steps can you take to keep your relationship with God fresh and vibrant, ensuring that you remain open to His leading and direction?** Consider how you can incorporate spiritual disciplines and intentional practices that foster growth and renewal in your walk with God.

Intentional blindness can hinder our spiritual growth and lead us into complacency. By seeking the Holy Spirit's guidance and embracing a life of faith and adventure, we can overcome routine and maintain a vibrant relationship with God. Let us pray for renewed vision and passion, trusting in God's promises and embracing the journey He has set before us.

Day 14
We are Transformers!

John 1:12 (AMP) "But as many as did receive and welcome Him, He gave the authority to become the children of God, that is to believe in His name."

The Power of Transformation

2 Corinthians 5:17 (NIV) - "Therefore, if anyone is in Christ, the new creation has come: The old has gone, the new is here!"

I still remember that night in June 2009 when I went with my family, staff, and interns to see the new Transformers movie. I was impressed by the technology of movie-making and how far it has advanced since the days of the Rocky movies.

As I was watching the movie, I realized that God made the first transformer—Adam. He created man in such detail and with such an ability to change that if he wanted to pull a woman out of his side, he could. It was out of Adam that God transformed man into a marriage, and from that marriage, He transformed man into a race. God never had to reach into the ground again to create because of the transformation power He gave to us. We are transformers!

Designed to Transform

Romans 12:2 (NIV) - "Do not conform to the pattern of this world, but be transformed by the renewing of your mind. Then you will be able to test and approve what God's will is—his good, pleasing and perfect will."

For the Christian, transformation at its optimum is the working out of the internal. God placed certain things in us that have to come out. The blueprint for a complete transformation is already in us. We were designed to transform and become the very thing He purposed us to be. We transform out of our old selves and into our character, purpose, and ministry. It's there; we just have to believe that it is.

As believers in Christ, our spiritual lives are similar to the caterpillar—we have been through a metamorphosis and continue to do so every day. We are in a continuous process of transformation. We seem to be out of the cocoon in some areas and sleeping away and eating in others.

The Power of Grace

2 Corinthians 12:9 (NIV) - "But he said to me, 'My grace is sufficient for you, for my power is made perfect in weakness.' Therefore I will boast all the more gladly about my weaknesses, so that Christ's power may rest on me."

When we received Christ and became born again, God ignited His power (**exousia**—right and authority) to become what the Lord has designed us to be! Salvation as it relates to your destiny is the God-given power to become what God has eternally decreed you were before the foundations of the earth! Salvation is the epitome of GRACE. Grace is God's divine enablement to accomplish and fulfill a predetermined purpose! **2 Corinthians 12:9** says, "My Grace is sufficient for you"—In other words, His power is not intimidated by your problems—you are already wired to overcome! You are designed to transform and become what you were designed to be.

Embracing Our Transformation

Philippians 1:6 (NIV) - "Being confident of this, that he who began a good work in you will carry it on to completion until the day of Christ Jesus."

Transformation is an ongoing journey that involves trusting God's plan and allowing His Spirit to work in us. As we embrace our transformation, we become more aligned with God's purposes and experience the fullness of life He intends for us. Our transformation is not just for our benefit but also for impacting the world around us.

Practical Application:

- Reflect on areas in your life where God is calling you to transform. Consider how you can actively participate in His work in you.

- Pray for God's grace and power to enable you to overcome challenges and become the person He designed you to be.

Application

Ephesians 2:10 (NIV) - "For we are God's handiwork, created in Christ Jesus to do good works, which God prepared in advance for us to do."

Reflect on your journey of transformation and how you can embrace God's work in your life. Consider how you can actively pursue the purpose and calling He has for you, trusting in His grace and power to guide you. Commit to being open to the changes God wants to make in you, knowing that He is faithful to complete the work He has begun.

Challenge Questions

1. **In what areas of your life do you feel God is calling you to transform, and how can you embrace His work in these areas?** Reflect on specific aspects of your character, purpose, or ministry where transformation is needed, and consider steps to align with God's plan.

2. **How can you rely on God's grace and power to overcome challenges and fulfill the purpose He has for you?** Identify ways to strengthen your reliance on God's grace and seek His guidance in every area of your life.

3. **What practical steps can you take to actively participate in your transformation, ensuring you become the person God designed you to be?** Consider how you can engage in spiritual disciplines, seek mentorship, and pursue opportunities for growth and service.

Transformation is a continuous journey that requires faith, grace, and a willingness to grow. By embracing God's work in our lives, we can become the people He designed us to be and fulfill our purpose in His Kingdom. Let us trust in His power and grace, knowing that we are transformers, continually being shaped and renewed by His Spirit.

Day 15

Are You Willing to Dress Up?

Matthew 22:8-10 (NIV) "Then he said to his servants, 'The wedding banquet is ready, but those I invited did not deserve to come. So go to the street corners and invite to the banquet anyone you find.' So the servants went out into the streets and gathered all the people they could find, the bad as well as the good, and the wedding hall was filled with guests.

Matthew 22:1-14 (NIV)

Jesus spoke to them again in parables, saying: "The kingdom of heaven is like a king who prepared a wedding banquet for his son. He sent his servants to those who had been invited to the banquet to tell them to come, but they refused to come.

"Then he sent some more servants and said, 'Tell those who have been invited that I have prepared my dinner: My oxen and fattened cattle have been slaughtered, and everything is ready. Come to the wedding banquet.'

"But they paid no attention and went off—one to his field, another to his business. The rest seized his servants, mistreated them, and killed them. The king was enraged. He sent his army and destroyed those murderers and burned their city.

"Then he said to his servants, 'The wedding banquet is ready, but those I invited did not deserve to come. So go to the street corners and invite to the banquet anyone you find.' So the servants went out into the streets and gathered all the people they could find, the bad as well as the good, and the wedding hall was filled with guests.

"But when the king came in to see the guests, he noticed a man there who was not wearing wedding clothes. He asked, 'How did you get in here without wedding clothes, friend?' The man was speechless.

"Then the king told the attendants, 'Tie him hand and foot, and throw him outside, into the darkness, where there will be weeping and gnashing of teeth.'

"For many are invited, but few are chosen."

The Invitation to the Kingdom

I've been studying the book of Matthew for quite some time now. It's intriguing to know the different viewpoints in this synoptic Gospel. The Word of God continues to amaze me in its depths and complexity and how it communicates God's principles, ethics, and morality.

The Parable of the Wedding Feast is a very interesting one. Though there is not enough space to type a commentary of this parable on this blog, let me point out some interesting points.

This parable is allegorically and metaphorically communicating the Gospel and salvation message. The king (representing God) invites people to the wedding feast for His Son, Jesus, but they refuse to come. So He does it again and again they refuse to come, but this time they kill His messengers. When the king heard about it, he was furious and made those people pay by destroying them and their city. So instead, He went out to the highways and byways and invited everyone that could come. The hall was filled with people, but when the king came in to see who was there, he noticed a man who did not have on a wedding garment. What happened? He was thrown out where there was weeping and gnashing of teeth.

Order and Obedience

John 14:15 (NIV) - "If you love me, keep my commands."

It's all about motives and agendas. Only God knows the condition of men's hearts. This parable is quite sobering to me. There are many principles to this parable, but what screams out to me is order and obedience. The man in the wedding without a wedding garment signifies a person desiring to be in the kingdom without wanting to follow the protocols of the kingdom. There was nothing significant about the clothing itself, only that they reflect the condition and motive of the hearts of men. We, as humans, want salvation and eternal life, but only on our terms and conditions. It's the man-made, idolatrous, self-justifying philosophy that has affected the church of today.

The Nature of True Worship

Romans 12:1 (NIV) - "Therefore, I urge you, brothers and sisters, in view of God's mercy, to offer your bodies as a living sacrifice, holy and pleasing to God—this is your true and proper worship."

God loves the world and He is forgiving and kind, but understand that He is still God. He is a king, and kings have rules, protocols, laws, commandments, and government. Our love for Him is not based on how we can justify our desires and actions to try to be part of His kingdom, rather on how we obey His rules and mandates according to His word.

After all, Jesus said, "…If you love me, you will obey my commandments." The message goes out to all, but the truth is that "...many are called but few are chosen."

Modern-Day Guests Without Wedding Clothes

The parable of the wedding feast can be applied to modern times by examining the types of people who may find themselves in the wedding hall without proper wedding attire. Here are some examples:

1. ***The Complacent Believer:*** Those who profess faith but lack a genuine commitment to follow God's commands. They go through the motions of religious activity without a true heart transformation.

2. ***The Self-Righteous:*** Individuals who believe they can earn their way into God's favor through good deeds or moral behavior, neglecting the necessity of grace and faith in Christ.

3. ***The Indifferent:*** People who attend church and hear the Gospel but remain unmoved, never allowing the message to penetrate their hearts and change their lives.

4. ***The Cultural Christian:*** Those who identify as Christians due to cultural or familial traditions but lack a personal relationship with Jesus and a desire to live according to His teachings.

Preparing for the Kingdom

Colossians 3:12-14 (NIV) - "Therefore, as God's chosen people, holy and dearly loved, clothe yourselves with compassion, kindness, humility, gentleness and patience. Bear with each other and forgive one another if any of you has a grievance against someone. Forgive as the Lord forgave you. And over all these virtues put on love, which binds them all together in perfect unity."

To be properly attired for the wedding feast, we must clothe ourselves with the virtues of Christ, aligning our lives with His teachings and embracing His grace. This involves a commitment to living out our faith authentically and intentionally, allowing God to transform us from the inside out.

Practical Application:

- Reflect on your own life and consider whether you are truly prepared to enter God's kingdom. Are you clothed in the virtues and character of Christ?

- Seek to grow in obedience and love for God, ensuring that your faith is genuine and rooted in a relationship with Him.

Application

2 Corinthians 13:5 (NIV) - "Examine yourselves to see whether you are in the faith; test yourselves. Do you not realize that Christ Jesus is in you—unless, of course, you fail the test?"

Reflect on your spiritual condition and consider how you can align your life with the teachings and commands of Christ. Ensure that you are properly attired for the wedding feast, living a life of obedience and love for God.

Challenge Questions

1.   **In what ways can you ensure that your faith is genuine and not merely a cultural or superficial expression?** Reflect on your relationship with God and consider steps to deepen your faith and commitment to Him.

2.   **How can you actively pursue the virtues and character of Christ in your daily life, ensuring that you are clothed in His righteousness?** Identify practical ways to grow in compassion, kindness, humility, and love, reflecting the image of Christ in your actions and attitudes.

3.   **What areas of your life may need transformation or repentance to align more closely with God's kingdom values and commands?** Consider how you can seek God's guidance and strength to make necessary changes and live a life that honors Him.

The parable of the wedding feast challenges us to examine our hearts and ensure that we are truly prepared for God's kingdom. By embracing the call to obedience and allowing God to transform us, we can be confident that we are clothed in His righteousness and ready to participate in the celebration of His eternal kingdom. Let us strive to live lives that reflect the love and grace of Christ, knowing that we are invited to the wedding feast as beloved children of God.

Day 16

My Personal Audit

2 Corinthians 13:5 (NIV) "Examine yourselves to see whether you are in the faith; test yourselves. Do you not realize that Christ Jesus is in you—unless, of course, you fail the test?"

The Importance of Self-Examination

Psalm 139:23-24 (NIV) - "Search me, God, and know my heart; test me and know my anxious thoughts. See if there is any offensive way in me, and lead me in the way everlasting."

Recently I conducted an audit of my walk with Christ and pursuit of His purpose in my life. Though I found many positive things, my mind leaned toward the things that needed much improvement. I realized, as I desired to reach new levels, I lacked in a few items. At first, I thought if I communicate them with you it would make me vulnerable, but then I recognized that the items listed below seem to be popular with everyone. So, here they are...

Conducting a personal audit is an essential part of spiritual growth. It allows us to assess where we are in our journey with Christ, identify areas for improvement, and realign our lives with God's purpose. This process of reflection and self-examination is crucial for nurturing a vibrant and fruitful relationship with God.

Lack of Knowledge

Proverbs 18:15 (NIV) - "The heart of the discerning acquires knowledge, for the ears of the wise seek it out."

- Wrong decisions in my life were made because of wrong information.

- Wrong information resulted in a lack of knowledge.

- Knowledge is not just a lack of information but also an inability to use it!

- **Hosea 4:6** - "My people are destroyed for a lack of knowledge."

- I must read more... Study more... Process more... Teach more....

- I refuse to be STUPID!

Knowledge is a vital component of our spiritual journey. It equips us to make wise decisions, understand God's will, and grow in our faith. A lack of knowledge can lead to poor choices and hinder our progress. To overcome this, we must commit to reading, studying, and teaching God's Word, ensuring that we are continually growing in understanding and wisdom.

A Lack of Passion

Philippians 3:13-14 (NIV) - "Brothers and sisters, I do not consider myself yet to have taken hold of it. But one thing I do: Forgetting what is behind and straining toward what is ahead, I press on toward the goal to win the prize for which God has called me heavenward in Christ Jesus."

• This means a lack of pursuit. Not desiring to pursue Him will cause me to stagnate and bog down into a survival stage.

• I MUST CONTINUE TO DREAM! If my dream does not inspire me, then it won't inspire others... If it doesn't get me out of bed, then it won't get anyone out of bed!

• Jesus, my example, was motivated to endure the cross because he had passion.

• My greatest responsibility as a Christian is to pursue God every day!

Passion is the driving force behind our pursuit of God and His purpose for our lives. Without passion, we risk stagnation and complacency. We must cultivate a passion for God's presence, allowing it to fuel our dreams and inspire others. Like Jesus, we are called to endure challenges with a steadfast focus on the joy set before us.

A Lack of Persistence

Galatians 6:9 (NIV) - "Let us not become weary in doing good, for at the proper time we will reap a harvest if we do not give up."

• I was designed to create solutions and to solve problems. Not accomplishing this is a problem in persistence.

• It will always be too soon to quit! I have realized that no one remembers quitters!

• I must HOLD firmly to my purpose regardless of how difficult the journey is!

• Persistence is what fuels my purpose! My purpose and destiny become achievable when it's fueled by persistence!

Persistence is essential for fulfilling our God-given purpose. It enables us to persevere through challenges, remain focused on our goals, and achieve our destiny. By holding firmly to our purpose and refusing to give up, we demonstrate faithfulness and resilience in our walk with Christ.

Embracing Growth and Transformation

Romans 12:2 (NIV) - "Do not conform to the pattern of this world, but be transformed by the renewing of your mind. Then you will be able to test and approve what God's will is—his good, pleasing and perfect will."

As we conduct personal audits and identify areas for growth, we open ourselves to God's transformative work in our lives. By seeking knowledge, cultivating passion, and embracing persistence, we align ourselves with God's purpose and experience the fullness of His grace and power.

Practical Application:

- Reflect on your own walk with Christ and consider areas where you may need to grow in knowledge, passion, or persistence.

- Set specific goals for growth in each area and commit to pursuing them with intentionality and dedication.

Application

2 Peter 1:5-8 (NIV) - "For this very reason, make every effort to add to your faith goodness; and to goodness, knowledge; and to knowledge, self-control; and to self-control, perseverance; and to perseverance, godliness; and to godliness, mutual affection; and to mutual affection, love. For if you possess these qualities in increasing measure, they will keep you from being ineffective and unproductive in your knowledge of our Lord Jesus Christ."

Reflect on how you can embrace growth and transformation in your walk with Christ. Consider how you can pursue knowledge, passion, and persistence, ensuring that you are continually growing in your relationship with God and fulfilling His purpose for your life.

Challenge Questions

1. **In what areas of your life do you need to grow in knowledge, and how can you actively seek understanding and wisdom in your walk with Christ?** Reflect on specific topics or areas where you lack knowledge, and consider steps to pursue growth through study and reflection.

2. **How can you cultivate a renewed passion for God and His purpose, ensuring that your faith is vibrant and inspiring to others?** Identify practical ways to reignite your passion for God's presence and mission, such as prayer, worship, and service.

3. **What steps can you take to embrace persistence in your journey, holding firmly to your purpose and refusing to give up despite challenges?** Consider how you can develop resilience and perseverance in your walk with Christ, relying on His strength and guidance.

Conducting a personal audit of our walk with Christ allows us to identify areas for growth and align our lives with God's purpose. By seeking knowledge, cultivating passion, and embracing persistence, we can experience transformation and fulfill the calling God has for us. Let us commit to growing in our relationship with God, trusting Him to lead us into greater levels of faith and purpose.

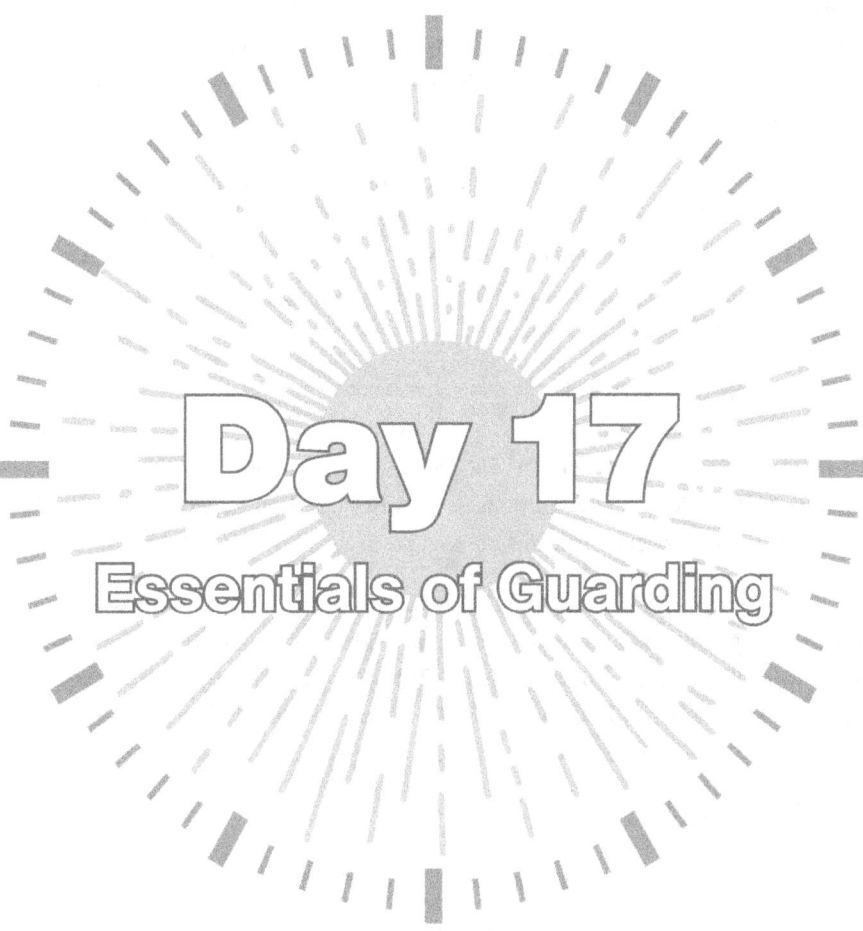

Day 17

Essentials of Guarding

Proverbs 4:23 (NIV) "Above all else, guard your heart, for it is the wellspring of life."

The Importance of Guarding

Philippians 4:7 (NIV) - "And the peace of God, which transcends all understanding, will guard your hearts and your minds in Christ Jesus."

In stewarding relationships in my life, I've always tried to find the balance between being defensive and being permissive. I've discovered that most people operate in the extreme and are either one or the other. The key is to guard. Guarding is simply having personal boundaries that others cannot cross unless given the pass to do so.

When people are permissive, they become vulnerable to the influences of others. Believe it or not, most of the decisions we make are not God-influenced; rather, they are man-influenced. When we become permissive in our relationships, we obviously become vulnerable to the wrong people who have the wrong voices. I call them destiny destroyers.

Learning to Guard

Psalm 48:12-13 (NIV) - "Walk about Zion, go around her, count her towers, consider well her ramparts, view her citadels, that you may tell of them to the next generation."

We must learn to guard. **Psalm 48:12-13** tells us the city of God had watchtowers, ramparts, and citadels. All these are designed to guard and be watchful. Jesus himself lived a guarded life. **John 2:24-25** states, *"But Jesus would not entrust himself to them, for he knew all men. He did not need man's testimony about man, for he knew what was in a man."* To guard is to create Godly boundaries.

Godly Boundaries

These Godly boundaries must be placed in four areas of our lives:

1. ***Talk Psalm 141:3 (NIV)*** - "Set a guard over my mouth, O LORD; keep watch over the door of my lips." We are to be selective with our communication; the type of personal information we receive and share with others. Our words have power and influence, and guarding our speech helps us protect our hearts and maintain integrity in our relationships.

2. **Time Proverbs 22:5 (NIV)** - "In the paths of the wicked lie thorns and snares, but he who guards his soul stays far from them." We must carefully predetermine and administer the time we spend with certain people. Time is the primary asset God has given us to invest. Guard it! By prioritizing our time wisely, we ensure that we are investing in relationships and activities that align with God's purpose.

3. **Touch Jeremiah 2:13 (NIV)** - "My people have committed two sins: They have forsaken me, the spring of living water, and have dug their own cisterns, broken cisterns that cannot hold water." Be careful and watchful as to who pours into your life. If they are pouring from a contaminated well, you too will be contaminated. We must be discerning about the influences we allow into our lives and seek relationships that nurture and uplift our faith.

4. **Tangibles Proverbs 12:27 (NIV)** - "The lazy man does not roast his game, but the diligent man prizes his possessions." Be watchful of the resources the Lord has given you. Don't share your belongings, especially your money, with people that don't qualify to cross your boundary, especially lazy people. Being wise stewards of our resources helps us honor God and use what He has entrusted to us for His glory.

Guarding Your Heart

Colossians 3:2 (NIV) - "Set your minds on things above, not on earthly things."

Guarding our hearts involves setting boundaries that protect us from negative influences and distractions. By focusing on God's Word and His promises, we cultivate a heart that is aligned with His will and purpose. Our relationships and decisions are guided by the principles of love, integrity, and wisdom.

Practical Application:

- Reflect on the areas of your life where boundaries may need to be established or strengthened. Consider how you can guard your heart and relationships more effectively.

- Seek God's guidance in prayer, asking Him to help you discern the influences and priorities in your life.

Application

Ephesians 6:10-11 (NIV) - "Finally, be strong in the Lord and in his mighty power. Put on the full armor of God, so that you can take your stand against the devil's schemes."

Reflect on how you can guard your heart and life with Godly boundaries, ensuring that your relationships and actions align with His will. Consider how you can protect your heart from negative influences and cultivate a life that honors God.

Challenge Questions

1.   **In what areas of your life do you need to establish or strengthen boundaries, and how can you protect your heart from negative influences?** Reflect on specific relationships or activities that may require boundaries, and consider steps to safeguard your heart and mind.

2.   **How can you ensure that your time and resources are invested in ways that align with God's purpose and bring glory to Him?** Identify practical ways to prioritize your time and use your resources wisely, seeking God's guidance in your decisions.

3.   **What steps can you take to guard your speech and ensure that your words reflect the love and integrity of Christ?** Consider how you can be intentional about your communication, speaking words that build up and encourage others.

Guarding our hearts is essential for living a life that honors God and fulfills His purpose. By establishing Godly boundaries in our relationships, time, speech, and resources, we protect ourselves from negative influences and align our lives with His will. Let us commit to guarding our hearts diligently, trusting God to guide us in every area of our lives.

Day 18
Christianity is One Big Verb!

Matthew 24:46 (NIV) "Blessed is that servant whom his master, when he comes, will find so doing."

The Essence of Eschatology

Matthew 24:42 (NIV) - "Therefore keep watch, because you do not know on what day your Lord will come."

Chapters 24-26 of the Gospel of Matthew are what we call eschatological. Eschatology is simply the study of the end times (end of the world) and our placement in it. This will forever be a very interesting subject. It has made multiple millions of dollars for those who believe they have an understanding of it; therefore, they write the books, create their graphs, send out newsletters, and broadcast their shows. I'm not saying that these people are peddling the gospel and marketing the mysteriousness of prophecies and end-times scripture. What bothers me is that they continually have to rewrite their books and predictions of prophecies and yet again, resell books, recreate graphs, rewrite newsletters, and rebroadcast shows.

Eschatology is a topic that fascinates many and sparks debates and discussions among scholars and believers. While it is important to study and understand the teachings of Scripture about the end times, it is equally important not to get lost in speculation and predictions. The true essence of eschatology is to encourage us to live in readiness and active service as we await Christ's return.

Focus on Active Faith

Matthew 25:13 (NIV) - "Therefore keep watch, because you do not know the day or the hour."

I've never been an eschatological preacher. Though the subject is intriguing, in 35 years of ministry, I have never attempted to teach or preach the interpretations of the prophecies. I get asked the question as to why I have not taught on the rapture or the second coming. Quite frankly, I stay away from the debate of a subject that its full understanding is not yet settled in its foundation. Have I studied it? Oh yes, very much. I have a good understanding of all the schools of thought about it. But what I do well is preach and teach on how to live successfully through the end times.

There is one defining principle in the three eschatological chapters of Matthew. It's not analyzing, looking, and wondering, but rather DOING! We must remain busy until Jesus comes back. Don't get distracted by all the rhetoric and philosophy; just keep preaching and living the gospel. Keep winning people to Christ. Be diligent and wise; make sure you always have enough oil in your lamps to recognize the coming of Christ. Keep your anointing fresh. Also, don't be lazy and wicked and bury your talents, rather invest them and put them to work for you. Our master is in heaven now, but when he returns, make sure you have multiplied what he has given you. Lastly, be sure to feed the hungry, quench the thirst of the thirsty, take in the stranger, clothe the naked, and visit the sick and the imprisoned; because if you do this to one of these, you do it unto Jesus.

Living Out the Gospel

James 2:17 (NIV) - "In the same way, faith by itself, if it is not accompanied by action, is dead."

Christianity is a verb! Don't look to the clouds wondering when he will return. Get busy. Let's get to work! Jesus emphasized the importance of active faith and service in His teachings. Our faith is not just about belief but also about action. We are called to be His hands and feet, serving others and sharing the love of Christ in tangible ways.

Being Prepared and Faithful

Matthew 25:21 (NIV) - "His master replied, 'Well done, good and faithful servant! You have been faithful with a few things; I will put you in charge of many things. Come and share your master's happiness!'"

Living in readiness for Christ's return involves being faithful stewards of what He has entrusted to us. Whether it's our time, talents, or resources, we are called to use them for His glory and the advancement of His Kingdom. By living out our faith actively and intentionally, we demonstrate our love for God and our commitment to His purposes.

Practical Application:

- Reflect on how you can actively live out your faith and serve others in your community. Consider how you can use your gifts and resources to make a difference.

- Commit to staying spiritually vigilant and prepared, focusing on growing in your relationship with God and serving His Kingdom.

Application

1 Corinthians 15:58 (NIV) - "Therefore, my dear brothers and sisters, stand firm. Let nothing move you. Always give yourselves fully to the work of the Lord, because you know that your labor in the Lord is not in vain."

Reflect on how you can embrace the call to active faith and service, ensuring that your life reflects the love and purpose of Christ. Consider how you can use your time, talents, and resources to impact others and glorify God.

Challenge Questions

1. **In what ways can you actively live out your faith and serve others, ensuring that you are fulfilling God's call in your life?** Reflect on specific opportunities or ministries where you can use your gifts and talents to serve and bless others.

2. **How can you stay spiritually vigilant and prepared for Christ's return, focusing on growing in your relationship with Him and advancing His Kingdom?** Identify practical ways to nurture your spiritual life and remain engaged in the work of the Gospel.

3. **What steps can you take to ensure that your faith is not just a belief but an active expression of love and service to those around you?** Consider how you can live out the teachings of Jesus in your daily interactions and commitments.

Christianity is a verb, calling us to live out our faith through action and service. As we await Christ's return, let us commit to being faithful stewards of what He has entrusted to us, actively serving others and sharing His love. By living with intentionality and purpose, we fulfill our calling and demonstrate the transformative power of the Gospel. Let us embrace the call to action, knowing that our labor in the Lord is not in vain.

Day 19

Why The Waste

Matthew 26:6-9 (NIV) "While Jesus was in Bethany in the home of a man known as Simon the Leper, a woman came to him with an alabaster jar of very expensive perfume, which she poured on his head as he was reclining at the table. When the disciples saw this, they were indignant. 'Why this waste?' they asked. 'This perfume could have been sold at a high price and the money given to the poor.'"

Lessons in Waste

> **Proverbs 21:20 (NIV)** - "The wise store up choice food and olive oil, but fools gulp theirs down."

Growing up as a middle child in a family of seven children taught me many things. Lessons, virtues, and concepts can be learned in a large family. I learned to be diplomatic, protective, and communal along with many other things. One virtue that was instilled in me was to never be wasteful. After all, in a household of nine (and sometimes visiting relatives), one cannot afford to waste anything.

I hate waste, any kind of waste. When something is wasted, it's discarded before its time and fulfillment of purpose, whether it's food, equipment, supplies, time, or money. But I believe the greatest waste there is the waste of a life.

In our text, we know that this perfume, though worth about a 40k salary, was not a waste but an act of worship by Mary. She literally poured out her most prized possession on Jesus. The disciples (predominantly Judas) could not see the value in her worship; all they saw was the amount of money they could have sold the alabaster for.

The Value of Worship

> **John 12:3-6 (NIV)** - "Then Mary took about a pint of pure nard, an expensive perfume; she poured it on Jesus' feet and wiped his feet with her hair. And the house was filled with the fragrance of the perfume. But one of his disciples, Judas Iscariot, who was later to betray him, objected, 'Why wasn't this perfume sold and the money given to the poor? It was worth a year's wages.' He did not say this because he cared about the poor but because he was a thief; as keeper of the money bag, he used to help himself to what was put into it."

According to the other gospels, it was Judas who exclaimed, "Why the waste?!" He, unfortunately, did not have an understanding of Jesus' mission and purpose. In a room full of men and disciples who have been with Jesus for 3½ years, it was a woman who lived a questionable lifestyle and was delivered from demons who recognized value. I wonder, who was really being wasteful? Was it Mary with her 40k offering or was it Judas with his life? Hmmm...

Mary's act of worship demonstrates that true value lies in our devotion to

Christ. Her willingness to pour out her most valuable possession reflects a heart fully surrendered to Jesus. In contrast, Judas's focus on the monetary value reveals a heart misaligned with God's purposes.

Making Life Count

Ephesians 5:15-17 (NIV) - "Be very careful, then, how you live—not as unwise but as wise, making the most of every opportunity, because the days are evil. Therefore do not be foolish, but understand what the Lord's will is."

The question is being asked: Are we wasting our lives or are we making them count? As a pastor, I'm learning to recognize when lives are being wasted. I hate waste. It frustrates me when lives are wasted and not used for the glory of God. I despise it when it occurs in my life.

So, be a "Mary!" Yes, people might think you're wasting your life as you pour out your life for the Kingdom of God. They will exclaim, like Judas, "Why the Waste!?" But please, don't be a "Judas," living your life pursuing your own agenda and selling out your friends, character, and values for profit. And if you are, then ask yourself, "Why the waste?"

Embracing God's Purpose

Philippians 3:7-8 (NIV) - "But whatever were gains to me I now consider loss for the sake of Christ. What is more, I consider everything a loss because of the surpassing worth of knowing Christ Jesus my Lord, for whose sake I have lost all things. I consider them garbage, that I may gain Christ."

Our lives are precious gifts from God, entrusted to us to fulfill His purposes. We must be intentional about how we use our time, resources, and talents, ensuring that they align with His will. By living for God's glory and pouring out our lives in worship, we find true fulfillment and make a lasting impact.

Practical Application:

- Reflect on how you can align your life with God's purposes and make every moment count for His Kingdom.

- Consider ways you can pour out your life in worship and service, offering your best to God.

Application

Colossians 3:23-24 (NIV) - "Whatever you do, work at it with all your heart, as working for the Lord, not for human masters, since you know that you will receive an inheritance from the Lord as a reward. It is the Lord Christ you are serving."

Reflect on how you can avoid wasting your life and ensure that your actions and priorities align with God's purposes. Consider how you can live a life of worship, devotion, and service to Christ, making the most of every opportunity to glorify Him.

Challenge Questions

1.   **In what ways can you ensure that your life is not wasted but used for God's glory and purposes?** Reflect on your current priorities and activities, and consider how you can align them with God's will.

2.   **How can you cultivate a heart of worship like Mary, willing to pour out your best for Christ regardless of the opinions of others?** Identify practical steps to deepen your devotion to God and express your love for Him in tangible ways.

3.   **What changes can you make to ensure that you are making the most of your time, talents, and resources for the Kingdom of God?** Consider how you can be intentional about your decisions and actions, focusing on eternal significance rather than temporary gain.

Living a life of worship and purpose requires us to align our hearts and actions with God's will. By embracing Mary's example and avoiding the pitfalls of wastefulness, we can make every moment count for His Kingdom. Let us commit to pouring out our lives in devotion to Christ, ensuring that we fulfill His purposes and bring glory to His name.

Day 20

Judas Iscariot

Matthew 26:25 (NIV) "Then Judas, the one who would betray him, said, 'Surely not I, Rabbi?' Jesus answered, 'Yes, it is you.'"

The Complexity of Judas's Choice

Matthew 26:14-16 (NIV) - "Then one of the Twelve—the one called Judas Iscariot—went to the chief priests and asked, 'What are you willing to give me if I deliver him over to you?' So they counted out for him thirty pieces of silver. From then on Judas watched for an opportunity to hand him over."

All the gospels give an account of the events that took place before Judas's betrayal of Christ. Much is said and debated of Judas's heart and motives. Some say it was his destiny and that he was placed there by God to robotically do what he did, and others say that he had a choice. I like to lean on the choice argument, even though God already knew beforehand. Yeah...I know...kinda weird, huh?

The story of Judas Iscariot challenges us to consider the nature of free will and divine foreknowledge. While God knew what Judas would do, Judas still made a conscious decision to betray Jesus. This raises questions about his internal struggle and the motivations that led to his ultimate decision.

The Inner Conflict

John 13:2 (NIV) - "The evening meal was in progress, and the devil had already prompted Judas, the son of Simon Iscariot, to betray Jesus."

It makes me wonder why Judas asked Jesus if it was he who was going to betray him. What was going through his mind? What was in his heart? The Bible specifically says that prior to this event Judas made arrangements to betray Jesus. Was he struggling not to follow through? I do know that once he made up his mind, the Bible tells us that Satan possessed him, and the rest was history.

Judas's question, "Surely not I, Rabbi?" reveals an internal conflict and a potential moment of hesitation. Despite his outward actions, there may have been a part of Judas that was torn between loyalty and betrayal. This internal battle is something we can all relate to in our spiritual journeys.

Reflecting on Our Own Hearts

Romans 3:23 (NIV) - "For all have sinned and fall short of the glory of God."

Aren't we all like Judases? Before you become self-righteous, please consider this... How often have we wrestled with temptations, justified our reasoning, and chosen to turn our backs on Him? Although it may not be an outward blatant denial, it's an internal denial not to keep covenant and to satisfy our own lust, desires, covetousness, envy, greed, cupidity, etc. In reality, we are not far off from Judas.

Each of us faces moments of weakness and temptation. We are all capable of making choices that betray our faith and values. Recognizing our own vulnerabilities helps us approach God with humility and a desire for transformation.

The Power of Confession and Repentance

1 John 1:9 (NIV) - "If we confess our sins, he is faithful and just and will forgive us our sins and purify us from all unrighteousness."

The difference makers here are confession and repentance. That is what separated David from Saul and Peter from Judas. Living a life of confession and repentance will give to us an assurance in which we won't have to ask the question Judas asked Jesus, "Surely not I, Rabbi?" No, we can function knowing very well that our hearts are set on Him but always understanding that we are only one thought away from being betrayers.

The stories of David and Peter remind us that repentance and a heart turned toward God can restore us from our failures. Unlike Judas, they chose to seek forgiveness and transformation, demonstrating that God's grace is available to all who turn to Him.

Living in Humility and Vigilance

1 Corinthians 10:12 (NIV) - "So, if you think you are standing firm, be careful that you don't fall!"

Remember, "Therefore, let him who thinks he stands take heed lest he fall." And pray every day, "...do not lead us into temptation, but deliver us from the evil one." (Luke 11:4)

Recognizing our potential for failure keeps us humble and dependent on God's guidance. By seeking His protection and strength, we can resist temptation and live faithfully according to His will.

Practical Application:

- Reflect on areas in your life where you may be struggling with temptation or betrayal of your values. Consider how you can turn to God in confession and repentance.

- Commit to seeking God's strength and guidance daily, asking Him to protect you from falling into sin.

Application

Psalm 51:10 (NIV) - "Create in me a pure heart, O God, and renew a steadfast spirit within me."

Reflect on how you can cultivate a heart of humility and vigilance, recognizing your need for God's grace and strength. Consider how you can live a life of confession and repentance, ensuring that your actions and decisions align with His will.

Challenge Questions

1.   **In what areas of your life do you struggle with temptation, and how can you seek God's strength to overcome them?** Reflect on specific situations where you may be vulnerable and consider steps to resist temptation and live faithfully.

2.   **How can you cultivate a lifestyle of confession and repentance, ensuring that you remain close to God and aligned with His will?** Identify practical ways to engage in regular self-reflection and seek God's forgiveness and guidance.

3.   **What steps can you take to live with humility and vigilance, recognizing your need for God's grace and protection?** Consider how you can incorporate prayer, accountability, and spiritual disciplines into your daily life.

The story of Judas Iscariot reminds us of our own vulnerabilities and the importance of confession and repentance. By recognizing our weaknesses and turning to God for strength, we can live faithfully and avoid the pitfalls of betrayal. Let us strive to cultivate hearts that are humble, vigilant, and fully devoted to Christ, trusting in His grace to guide us in every step of our journey.

Day 21
The Second Wind

Galatians 6:9 (NIV) "Let us not become weary in doing good, for at the proper time we will reap a harvest if we do not give up."

Understanding Weariness

Isaiah 40:29-31 (NIV) - "He gives strength to the weary and increases the power of the weak. Even youths grow tired and weary, and young men stumble and fall; but those who hope in the Lord will renew their strength. They will soar on wings like eagles; they will run and not grow weary, they will walk and not be faint."

Weariness is the primary enemy of the believer who has captured purpose and has an understanding of destiny. Before the demonic kingdom can ever manipulate, distort, and influence, weariness must take place. Weariness has many siblings: exhaustion, fatigue, apathy, and discouragement. The antithesis to weariness is restfulness and peacefulness. We must learn to forecast the symptoms of weariness for fear that they disqualify us from our purpose.

Weariness can creep in slowly, draining our energy and enthusiasm for the tasks God has set before us. It can manifest as physical fatigue, emotional exhaustion, or spiritual apathy. Recognizing the signs of weariness allows us to take proactive steps to combat it and remain faithful in our calling.

The Enemy of Passion

Matthew 11:28 (NIV) - "Come to me, all you who are weary and burdened, and I will give you rest."

The greatest enemy to passion is weariness. Jesus said in Matthew 11:28, "Come to me, all you who are weary and burdened, and I will give you rest." The word weary in its Greek context is kopiaō, meaning, to grow weary, tired, exhausted (with toil or burdens or grief) to labor with wearisome effort, to toil. It is obvious that Jesus gives us the answer to weariness—His rest. His rest is not a rest of idleness and inactivity, but rather a rest during activity, commonly mentioned as a "second wind." A second wind is simply an acclimation to the resistance of our environment. It's the ability to overcome and have rest in the midst of the work.

Jesus invites us to find rest in Him, not by ceasing from our work but by relying on His strength and presence. His rest rejuvenates our spirit, enabling us to continue with renewed energy and focus. This second wind empowers us to persevere in our tasks and maintain our passion for God's work.

Finding Rest in Christ

Psalm 62:1-2 (NIV) - "Truly my soul finds rest in God; my salvation comes from him. Truly he is my rock and my salvation; he is my fortress, I will never be shaken."

Jesus said, come unto Him…it is when we are with Him that we remain restful in labor and in pursuit of fruitfulness. This keeps our passion active and with intentionality. There is no magic formula to this, bottom line—when we grow weary and exhausted, it's when we operate in our own very limited and finite strength. But when we remain in Him and function in His strength; a harvest of fruitfulness and success awaits us.

Finding rest in Christ involves surrendering our burdens and trusting Him to provide the strength we need. It requires us to prioritize time in His presence, seeking His guidance and allowing Him to refresh our souls. In doing so, we can experience the peace and rest that only He can provide.

Embracing the Second Wind

Philippians 4:13 (NIV) - "I can do all this through him who gives me strength."

The second wind is a gift from God, enabling us to push through challenges and continue in our purpose. As we rely on His strength, we discover the resilience and endurance needed to fulfill our calling. By embracing this divine empowerment, we can overcome weariness and achieve the harvest God has promised.

Practical Application:

• Reflect on areas of your life where you may be experiencing weariness. Consider how you can turn to Christ for rest and renewal.

• Commit to spending time in prayer and meditation, seeking God's presence and strength to overcome weariness and maintain passion for His work.

Application

Colossians 3:23-24 (NIV) - "Whatever you do, work at it with all your heart, as working for the Lord, not for human masters, since you know that you will receive an inheritance from the Lord as a reward. It is the Lord Christ you are serving."

Reflect on how you can embrace the second wind in your spiritual journey, relying on Christ's strength to overcome weariness and pursue His purpose with passion. Consider how you can remain steadfast in your calling, trusting that God's rest will sustain you.

Challenge Questions

1.   **In what areas of your life are you experiencing weariness, and how can you turn to Christ for rest and renewal?** Reflect on specific challenges or burdens you face, and consider how you can seek God's strength to persevere.

2.   **How can you cultivate a lifestyle of reliance on Christ's strength, ensuring that you remain passionate and purposeful in your work for His Kingdom?** Identify practical ways to integrate prayer, worship, and rest into your daily routine, allowing God to refresh and empower you.

3.   **What steps can you take to embrace the second wind, using it to overcome obstacles and achieve the harvest God has promised?** Consider how you can trust in God's provision and guidance, knowing that He equips you for the tasks He has called you to fulfill.

The second wind is a reminder of God's faithfulness and provision, empowering us to overcome weariness and continue in His purpose. By finding rest in Christ and relying on His strength, we can persevere in our calling and achieve the harvest He has promised. Let us embrace this divine empowerment, trusting that God will sustain us as we work for His Kingdom.

Day 22
What Motivates You?

Ephesians 3:20 (NIV) "Now to Him who is able to do exceedingly abundantly above all that we ask or think, according to the power that works in us…"

The Source of Motivation

Proverbs 4:23 (NIV) - "Above all else, guard your heart, for everything you do flows from it."

Any kind of success first begins with personal motivation. Motivation is simply the internal condition that activates behavior and gives it direction. Motivation is an impulse or a driving force that stems from an internal state of being. In other words, the motivation of your life derives from the most inward condition of your heart. Whatever rules your heart will motivate your life in its behaviors, actions, and reactions.

Motivation plays a crucial role in shaping our actions and decisions. It influences how we approach challenges, pursue goals, and respond to opportunities. Understanding what motivates us is essential for aligning our lives with God's purpose and experiencing His transformative power.

Partnering with God's Principles

John 3:30 (NIV) - "He must become greater; I must become less."

God can only operate in our lives according to how we partner and cooperate with His principles. Our motivation should only be the total submission to the will of God in our lives. John the Baptist said it best, "…I must decrease and He must increase." It's called living inside out.

When we live inside out, we live not according to extrinsic motivation, based on external conditions like riches, rewards, applause, etc., but rather intrinsic motivation based on self-discipline, conviction, and submission. Intrinsic motivation is simply the resident internal power of the Holy Spirit operating in us, thus causing us to connect with all He has for us. This power is simply a passion to give all of who we are to Him—a total surrender to His Lordship.

Intrinsic Motivation and Spiritual Growth

Philippians 2:13 (NIV) - "For it is God who works in you to will and to act in order to fulfill his good purpose."

Intrinsic motivation is the driving force that comes from within, rooted in our relationship with God and our desire to fulfill His purposes. It is fueled by the Holy Spirit, empowering us to pursue God's will with passion and dedication. When we are intrinsically motivated, our actions are driven by a deep love for God and a commitment to His Kingdom.

The Power at Work Within Us

Colossians 1:29 (NIV) - "To this end I strenuously contend with all the energy Christ so powerfully works in me."

Let us remember that the promise given to us is conditional…"according to the power that works in us." In other words, according to our internal motivation, God can work in our lives in an exceedingly abundantly above all that we ask or think fashion. And our success will be imminent. So…what is your internal condition? What motivates you? What drives you? What leads you? Is it extrinsic or intrinsic?

God's power at work within us is limitless, but it requires our cooperation and willingness to align our motivations with His purposes. By nurturing intrinsic motivation, we position ourselves to experience God's abundant blessings and achieve success in His Kingdom.

Cultivating Intrinsic Motivation

Romans 12:11 (NIV) - "Never be lacking in zeal, but keep your spiritual fervor, serving the Lord."

To cultivate intrinsic motivation, we must prioritize our relationship with God and seek His guidance in all areas of our lives. This involves spending time in prayer, studying His Word, and allowing the Holy Spirit to shape our desires and motivations. By focusing on God's will and surrendering our lives to Him, we can experience the joy and fulfillment that come from living according to His purposes.

Practical Application:

- Reflect on your current motivations and consider whether they are primarily extrinsic or intrinsic. Identify areas where you may need to realign your motivations with God's will.

- Commit to spending time in prayer and seeking God's guidance, asking Him to cultivate a heart that is motivated by His love and purposes.

Application

2 Corinthians 5:14-15 (NIV) - "For Christ's love compels us, because we are convinced that one died for all, and therefore all died. And he died for all, that those who live should no longer live for themselves but for him who died for them and was raised again."

Reflect on how you can cultivate intrinsic motivation in your spiritual journey, ensuring that your actions and decisions are driven by a love for God and a commitment to His purposes. Consider how you can align your life with God's will, allowing His power to work through you abundantly.

Challenge Questions

1.   **What currently motivates you in your spiritual journey, and how can you ensure that your motivations align with God's purposes?** Reflect on your motivations and consider how you can nurture a heart that is motivated by love for God and His Kingdom.

2.   **How can you cultivate intrinsic motivation, allowing the Holy Spirit to guide your actions and decisions?** Identify practical steps to deepen your relationship with God and seek His guidance in all areas of your life.

3.   **What changes can you make to ensure that your motivations are rooted in God's love and purpose, rather than external rewards or recognition?** Consider how you can focus on serving God and others, prioritizing His will over worldly motivations.

Understanding and cultivating the right motivations in our spiritual journey is essential for experiencing God's transformative power and fulfilling His purposes. By aligning our motivations with God's will and relying on His strength, we can live lives that are abundant, impactful, and pleasing to Him. Let us strive to cultivate intrinsic motivation, allowing God's love and power to work through us in all that we do.

Day 23
Fire in the Belly

Revelation 2:3-4 (NIV) "You have persevered and have endured hardships for my name, and have not grown weary. Yet I hold this against you: You have forsaken your first love. Remember the height from which you have fallen! Repent and do the things you did at first."

Rekindling Our First Love

1 Corinthians 13:2 (NIV) - "If I have the gift of prophecy and can fathom all mysteries and all knowledge, and if I have a faith that can move mountains, but do not have love, I am nothing."

The church of Ephesus was a very solid church. After all, the Apostle Paul planted it during a supernatural revival. The church was a strong and continuous congregation. They revitalized the city and changed many generations. They were relentless in their defense of the truth and carried the qualities of endurance and perseverance. But unfortunately, all the accolades were ignored by one complaint from Christ, "You have forsaken your first love." The mechanics of ministry and life replaced the passion of their relationship with God. Their love of success became their failure. They lost their passion!

The message to the church in Ephesus serves as a powerful reminder of the importance of maintaining our passion for God. No matter how strong or successful we appear to be, if we lose our first love, we risk becoming disconnected from the true source of our strength and purpose.

The Importance of Passion

Colossians 3:23 (NIV) - "Whatever you do, work at it with all your heart, as working for the Lord, not for human masters."

I've been on the subject of passion for some time now. It began in our leadership meeting three weeks ago, and I can't seem to shake it! Here are some more thoughts:

- Passion is the first step to any goal, objective, or aspiration.
- Passion differentiates those with a passing interest from those that are true activists.
- Passion is often the deciding factor between average and exceptional; the difference between mediocre and memorable.
- Passion is that "fire in the belly" that secedes mere competitors from champions.

Passion is the driving force that compels us to pursue God's calling with zeal and determination. It sets us apart and fuels our efforts, enabling us to overcome challenges and achieve greatness. Without passion, our actions become routine and lack the vibrant energy needed to make a lasting impact.

Keeping the Fire Burning

2 Timothy 1:6 (NIV) - "For this reason I remind you to fan into flame the gift of God, which is in you through the laying on of my hands."

Keep it simple. Keep it focused. Keep it real. So many things can diminish passion. Let passion burn! Stay the course!

Rekindling our passion requires intentional effort and focus. We must guard against complacency and distractions that can extinguish our enthusiasm. By staying connected to God through prayer, worship, and fellowship, we can fan the flames of passion and remain committed to His purposes.

Restoring Passion Through Repentance

Psalm 51:10 (NIV) - "Create in me a pure heart, O God, and renew a steadfast spirit within me."

When we find ourselves losing our first love, the path to restoration begins with repentance. Acknowledging our need for renewal and seeking God's forgiveness allows us to realign our hearts with His will. As we return to our first love, we can experience a renewed sense of passion and purpose.

Practical Application:

• Reflect on your current level of passion for God and His work. Consider areas where you may have lost your first love and need to rekindle your enthusiasm.

• Commit to spending intentional time in prayer and worship, seeking God's presence and allowing Him to reignite your passion.

Application

Romans 12:11 (NIV) - "Never be lacking in zeal, but keep your spiritual fervor, serving the Lord."

Reflect on how you can cultivate and maintain your passion for God's work, ensuring that your actions are driven by love and devotion. Consider how you can stay focused on your first love and remain committed to His calling.

Challenge Questions

1.   **In what areas of your life have you lost your first love, and how can you take steps to reignite your passion for God?** Reflect on specific aspects of your spiritual journey where passion has diminished, and consider how you can restore your enthusiasm.

2.   **How can you cultivate a lifestyle that prioritizes passion for God and His Kingdom, ensuring that your actions are driven by love and purpose?** Identify practical ways to nurture your relationship with God and stay connected to His presence and guidance.

3.   **What steps can you take to guard against complacency and distractions that can extinguish your passion, ensuring that you remain focused on God's calling?** Consider how you can create a supportive environment that encourages spiritual growth and maintains your zeal for God's work.

Passion is a vital component of our spiritual journey, empowering us to pursue God's calling with enthusiasm and dedication. By rekindling our first love and maintaining our focus on Him, we can experience the joy and fulfillment that come from living with purpose. Let us strive to keep the fire in our belly burning brightly, ensuring that our lives reflect the passion and love of Christ.

Day 24
Keeping it Real

Romans 12:9 (NIV) "Love must be sincere. Hate what is evil; cling to what is good."

The Power of Authenticity

John 4:23-24 (NIV) - "Yet a time is coming and has now come when the true worshipers will worship the Father in the Spirit and in truth, for they are the kind of worshipers the Father seeks. God is spirit, and his worshipers must worship in the Spirit and in truth."

G. Campbell Morgan told the story of the great English theatre actor named Macready. A preacher once asked him a question: "I wish you would explain to me something. What is the reason for the difference between you and me? You are appearing before crowds night after night with fiction, and the crowds come wherever you go. I am preaching the fundamental and unchangeable truth, and I am not getting any crowds at all." Macready's answer was this: "This is quite simple. I can tell you the difference between us. I present my fiction as though it were truth; you present your truth as though it were fiction." – OUCH!!

I heard Mario Murillo say it this way: "The reason more people go to the movies than attend church is because Hollywood can take what is NOT real and make it look real, and the Church takes what is REAL and make it look NOT REAL."

Authenticity is a powerful force that can captivate and inspire those around us. When we live with authenticity, we demonstrate the truth of the Gospel in a way that is compelling and relatable. Our faith becomes more than just words; it becomes a living testimony of God's transformative power.

The Importance of Keeping It Real

2 Corinthians 4:2 (NIV) - "Rather, we have renounced secret and shameful ways; we do not use deception, nor do we distort the word of God. On the contrary, by setting forth the truth plainly we commend ourselves to everyone's conscience in the sight of God."

We often use the term, "keep it real," and in doing so, will require a tremendous focus. "Keeping it real" is a simplification and continual maintenance of the vision and purpose of our hearts. By default, we tend to clutter our lives with all sorts of distractions and disruptions. And the ability to keep them at bay is the integrity of "keeping it real." But failure to do so is the very behavior of taking what is real and making it look like fiction.

Living authentically requires intentional focus and effort. It means being honest with ourselves and others about our struggles and victories, allowing God's truth to shine through every aspect of our lives. By keeping it real, we demonstrate the power and relevance of the Gospel in a world that is often skeptical and searching for answers.

The Essence of Passion and Purpose

Philippians 3:13-14 (NIV) - "Brothers and sisters, I do not consider myself yet to have taken hold of it. But one thing I do: Forgetting what is behind and straining toward what is ahead, I press on toward the goal to win the prize for which God has called me heavenward in Christ Jesus."

The essence of what burns on the inside ultimately determines what is accomplished on the outside. And a passion for your promise, your vision, or your goals will ultimately be reflected from your life. Remember, you are a billboard to everyone. Your life is a message. The world needs to see and hear REAL people with REAL challenges overcome because of a REAL God – who Really loves us and REALLY wants us to have REAL PASSION.

Our passion and purpose are rooted in our relationship with God and our desire to fulfill His calling in our lives. When we live with passion, we inspire others to pursue their own God-given dreams and goals. By keeping our focus on what truly matters, we can make a lasting impact and reflect the authenticity of our faith.

Living Authentically for Christ

1 Peter 3:15 (NIV) - "But in your hearts revere Christ as Lord. Always be prepared to give an answer to everyone who asks you to give the reason for the hope that you have. But do this with gentleness and respect."

Living authentically for Christ means being genuine in our interactions, transparent in our struggles, and passionate about sharing the hope we have in Him. It involves being a living testimony of God's love and grace, allowing others to see the reality of His presence in our lives.

Practical Application:

- Reflect on areas in your life where you may struggle with authenticity. Consider how you can keep it real in your relationships and interactions.

- Commit to seeking God's guidance in living authentically, allowing His truth to shape your thoughts, words, and actions.

Application

Colossians 3:17 (NIV) - "And whatever you do, whether in word or deed, do it all in the name of the Lord Jesus, giving thanks to God the Father through him."

Reflect on how you can live authentically for Christ, ensuring that your actions and words reflect the truth and power of the Gospel. Consider how you can inspire others through your genuine passion and commitment to God's purposes.

Challenge Questions

1. **In what areas of your life do you struggle with authenticity, and how can you seek God's guidance to live more genuinely?** Reflect on specific situations where you may feel tempted to present a false image and consider how you can align your actions with God's truth.

2. **How can you cultivate a lifestyle that prioritizes authenticity and passion for God, ensuring that your faith is both real and impactful?** Identify practical ways to nurture your relationship with God and demonstrate His love and grace in your daily interactions.

3. **What steps can you take to inspire others through your authentic faith and passion for God, making a lasting impact in your community and beyond?** Consider how you can share your testimony and experiences with others, encouraging them to pursue their own relationship with Christ.

Living authentically for Christ requires intentional focus and dedication, allowing God's truth to shine through every aspect of our lives. By keeping it real and maintaining our passion for God's purposes, we can make a meaningful impact and inspire others to embrace the reality of the Gospel. Let us strive to live with authenticity and passion, reflecting the love and grace of our Savior in all that we do.

Day 25
Covenant Community

Acts 2:42-44 (NIV) "They devoted themselves to the apostles' teaching and to fellowship, to the breaking of bread and to prayer. Everyone was filled with awe at the many wonders and signs performed by the apostles. All the believers were together and had everything in common."

The Need for Covenant Community

Hebrews 10:24-25 (NIV) - "And let us consider how we may spur one another on toward love and good deeds, not giving up meeting together, as some are in the habit of doing, but encouraging one another—and all the more as you see the Day approaching."

Times are changing for the church in the United States. Although many churches are growing and many people are being won to Christ, the anti-Christ spirit is increasing as well. We've reached an era, for the first time, when we are no longer defined as a Christian nation. We are approaching years of battle and persecution. That is why it's important that we become a covenant community. The notion of "church" must change from a casual place where we choose to attend when we feel like it to an essential, indispensable, and non-negotiable COVENANT COMMUNITY!

As the cultural landscape shifts, the church must adapt by strengthening its bonds and commitment to one another. A covenant community is characterized by deep relationships, shared values, and mutual support, providing a foundation for believers to thrive in times of challenge and persecution.

Characteristics of Covenant Community

Acts 4:32 (NIV) - "All the believers were one in heart and mind. No one claimed that any of their possessions was their own, but they shared everything they had."

The church in Acts aptly portrays what it means to be brought together in covenant community.

- *Acts 1:14* – continued in one accord...

- *Acts 2:1* – they were all in one accord...

- *Acts 2:41* – they were added unto them...

- *Acts 2:44* – all that believed were together...

- *Acts 2:46* – so continuing daily with one accord in the temple, and in breaking of bread from house to house...

Definition of Community: A society of people having common rights and privileges, common interests, living under the same laws and regulations, having a community spirit.

The Biblical concept of covenant community is depicted in the following statements:

- **Corporate Concern:** When people are more concerned with the corporate body than with themselves. **Acts 4:32**

- **Deep Relationships:** Individuals are being knitted, built, framed, and joined together. This speaks of close, long-lasting real friendships.

- **Spirit of Sacrifice:** The spirit of sacrifice becomes the attitude in which the church (covenant community) meets the needs of all.

- **Team Ministry:** When team ministry is properly implemented to meet the needs of the church and the community.

- **Godly Authority:** When the elderly retain the proper godly authority throughout their lives.

- **Gospel Focus:** Where the preaching of the Gospel and discipleship of people becomes the primary focus for every family.

Building a Strong Community

Ephesians 4:15-16 (NIV) - "Instead, speaking the truth in love, we will grow to become in every respect the mature body of him who is the head, that is, Christ. From him, the whole body, joined and held together by every supporting ligament, grows and builds itself up in love, as each part does its work."

Building a covenant community requires intentional effort and commitment. It involves fostering an environment where relationships are prioritized, needs are met through sacrificial love, and the Gospel remains central. By coming together as one body, the church can effectively navigate challenges and fulfill its mission.

The Impact of Covenant Community

John 13:34-35 (NIV) - "A new command I give you: Love one another. As I have loved you, so you must love one another. By this everyone will know that you are my disciples if you love one another."

A strong covenant community serves as a powerful witness to the world. It demonstrates the love and unity that Christ desires for His followers, drawing others to the truth of the Gospel. By living out our faith in authentic relationships, we can impact our communities and advance God's Kingdom.

Practical Application:

• Reflect on your current involvement in your church community. Consider how you can contribute to building a covenant community that prioritizes relationships and Gospel-centered living.

• Commit to investing in meaningful relationships within your church, seeking opportunities to serve and support one another.

Application

Colossians 3:12-14 (NIV) - "Therefore, as God's chosen people, holy and dearly loved, clothe yourselves with compassion, kindness, humility, gentleness, and patience. Bear with each other and forgive one another if any of you has a grievance against someone. Forgive as the Lord forgave you. And over all these virtues put on love, which binds them all together in perfect unity."

Reflect on how you can contribute to building a covenant community within your church, focusing on love, unity, and mutual support. Consider how you can foster deep relationships and prioritize the Gospel in your interactions.

Challenge Questions

1. **In what ways can you actively contribute to building a covenant community within your church, ensuring that relationships are deep and meaningful?** Reflect on your current involvement in your church community and consider how you can invest in relationships and support one another.

2. **How can you cultivate a spirit of sacrifice and service, meeting the needs of others within your community and advancing the Gospel?** Identify practical ways to serve and support others, demonstrating the love and unity that Christ desires for His followers.

3. **What steps can you take to ensure that the Gospel remains central in your community, guiding your interactions and relationships with others?** Consider how you can prioritize Gospel-centered living and discipleship, encouraging others to grow in their faith and impact their communities.

Building a covenant community is essential for navigating the challenges and opportunities of our changing times. By prioritizing relationships, sacrificial love, and the Gospel, the church can become a powerful witness to the world, demonstrating the truth and love of Christ. Let us commit to building strong, authentic communities that reflect God's Kingdom and advance His purposes.

Day 26
The Power of Partnerships

Philippians 1:5-7 (NIV) "In all my prayers for all of you, I always pray with joy because of your partnership in the gospel from the first day until now, being confident of this, that he who began a good work in you will carry it on to completion until the day of Christ Jesus. It is right for me to feel this way about all of you, since I have you in my heart; for whether I am in chains or defending and confirming the gospel, all of you share in God's grace with me."

The Desire for Growth and Partnership

Ecclesiastes 4:9-10 (NIV) - "Two are better than one, because they have a good return for their labor: If either of them falls down, one can help the other up. But pity anyone who falls and has no one to help them up."

I have not met anyone, as of yet, who did not have a desire to live life at another level. Humanity has within itself a desire to increase and upgrade in levels, whether it be spiritual, social, educational, creative, or financial. It does not matter what level of life we desire to upgrade to; the key to achieving this is in partnership.

Human beings naturally seek growth and advancement. We long for deeper connections, greater understanding, and increased influence. Partnerships play a critical role in helping us reach these new levels by providing support, encouragement, and resources that we cannot obtain alone.

The Importance of Relationships

Proverbs 27:17 (NIV) - "As iron sharpens iron, so one person sharpens another."

It is impossible to increase in life without a partnership. Partnerships are more than a mere business agreement. Partnerships are relationships. These relationships may be direct or indirect; they may be a close friendship or a distant mentor. I've heard this saying many times; not sure where it came from… "If you see a turtle on top of a fence post, know that it did not get there on its own." The fact is that we cannot get to where we desire without the partnership of relationships.

Partnerships are essential for personal and spiritual growth. They involve collaboration and mutual support, allowing us to learn from others and benefit from their experiences and wisdom. Whether through mentorship, friendship, or collaboration, partnerships help us navigate challenges and achieve our goals.

Partnership in the Gospel

1 Corinthians 12:12-13 (NIV) - "Just as a body, though one, has many parts, but all its many parts form one body, so it is with Christ. For we were all baptized by one Spirit so as to form one body—whether Jews or Gentiles, slave or free—and we were all given the one Spirit to drink."

The apostle Paul prayed with joy because of the partnership the Philippian church had with the Gospel. The church had a mutual understanding with the ministry of the apostle. They discovered how to increase in levels. They were at a level where most pastors dream of taking their church. They had "it." It was an understanding and embracing of the partnership they had with their purpose, the Gospel of Jesus.

The Holy Spirit wrote through Paul, "…being confident of this, that he who began a good work in you will carry it on to completion until the day of Christ Jesus." That "good work" is the partnership we have with the Gospel. The word partnership is the word "koinonia," which is a participation, social intercourse, benefaction, communication, and fellowship. The promise is that God will finish that "Good Work" in our lives. He will continue to increase us day by day, month by month, and year by year as long as we operate within our partnership.

The Impact of Partnerships

Proverbs 13:20 (NIV) - "Walk with the wise and become wise, for a companion of fools suffers harm."

You are who you are because of your partnerships—good or bad. So whatever you do, stay connected to your church. Get in partnership with Christ, the vision of His church, and the people who pour into your life. It's impossible to increase in life without partnerships.

Our partnerships influence our growth and success. By surrounding ourselves with people who share our values and vision, we create an environment that fosters growth and encourages us to reach our full potential. These partnerships help us stay connected to our purpose and remain focused on God's calling.

Practical Application:

• Reflect on your current partnerships and consider how they are influencing your growth and success. Identify any relationships that may need strengthening or adjustment.

• Commit to building and nurturing partnerships that align with your values and support your spiritual and personal growth.

Application

Hebrews 10:24-25 (NIV) - "And let us consider how we may spur one another on toward love and good deeds, not giving up meeting together, as some are in the habit of doing, but encouraging one another—and all the more as you see the Day approaching."

Reflect on how you can actively engage in partnerships that support your growth and success, ensuring that your relationships align with God's purposes. Consider how you can contribute to and benefit from these partnerships, fostering an environment of mutual support and encouragement.

Challenge Questions

1. **In what ways can you strengthen your partnerships within your church and community, ensuring that they support your spiritual growth and development?** Reflect on your current relationships and consider how you can invest in partnerships that align with your values and goals.

2. **How can you actively engage in partnerships that promote collaboration and mutual support, helping you achieve your personal and spiritual aspirations?** Identify practical steps to build and nurture partnerships that encourage growth and foster a sense of community.

3. **What steps can you take to ensure that your partnerships are rooted in the Gospel and reflect the values of God's Kingdom?** Consider how you can prioritize Gospel-centered relationships and work together to advance God's purposes.

The power of partnerships lies in their ability to support and encourage us in our spiritual and personal journeys. By engaging in relationships that align with our values and goals, we can grow and thrive, fulfilling God's purposes for our lives. Let us commit to building strong, Gospel-centered partnerships that foster mutual support and advance His Kingdom

Day 27
Every Joint Supplies

Ephesians 4:16 (NIV) "From whom the whole body, joined and knit together by what every joint supplies, according to the effective working by which every part does its share, causes growth of the body for the edifying of itself in love."

The Importance of Unity in the Church

1 Corinthians 12:12-14 (NIV) - "Just as a body, though one, has many parts, but all its many parts form one body, so it is with Christ. For we were all baptized by one Spirit so as to form one body—whether Jews or Gentiles, slave or free—and we were all given the one Spirit to drink. Even so the body is not made up of one part but of many."

The overall health of a church is determined not by how its members can preach, teach, sing, counsel, and motivate, but by its relationships and bonds with each other. Notice, Paul does not say, "by what every part or member supplies," but "every joint supplies." The secret is in the joints! This is how we know we have a healthy body.

The effectiveness and growth of the church depend on the unity and strength of its relationships. Each member plays a crucial role, but it is the connections between members that allow the church to function as a cohesive and powerful force for God's Kingdom.

The Analogy of the Body

Romans 12:4-5 (NIV) - "For just as each of us has one body with many members, and these members do not all have the same function, so in Christ we, though many, form one body, and each member belongs to all the others."

Paul uses our physical bodies as an analogy. And in his time, medical studies had not reached a point of understanding the human body. But the Holy Spirit, who knows all things, gave us this physical and spiritual truth. You see, the growth plate, also known as the physis, is the area of developing tissue at the joints of the long bones in children and adolescents. Each long bone has at least two growth plates: one at each end or joint. This growth plate determines the future length and shape of the mature bone. In other words, the healthy growth of the church is determined by the health of its joints (relationships, bonds, friendships, etc).

The analogy of the body illustrates the interconnectedness of believers within the church. Just as the physical body relies on healthy joints for growth and movement, the church relies on strong relationships and connections to thrive and fulfill its mission.

The Power of Relationships

Colossians 2:19 (NIV) - "They have lost connection with the head, from whom the whole body, supported and held together by its ligaments and sinews, grows as God causes it to grow."

So, how many joints are there in a body? The smallest body of people consists of two members, who can form only one joint (or one bond, one relationship). A body of three members has three possible joints, and a body of four members has six possible joints. Five members means ten joints, six members amount to fifteen possible joints.

Notice how the number of possible joints increases much faster than the number of members! Among ten members, forty-five joints are possible; among fifty members, 1,222 joints! For a body of one hundred members to be "joined and knit together" requires more than 5,000 joints! The more the joints, the greater the flexibility! The greater the flexibility, the greater the ability to solve problems and accomplish more!

The strength and effectiveness of a church are amplified by the number and quality of its relationships. By fostering strong connections and unity among members, the church becomes more adaptable, resilient, and capable of achieving its goals and mission.

Demonstrating Love and Unity

John 13:34-35 (NIV) - "A new command I give you: Love one another. As I have loved you, so you must love one another. By this everyone will know that you are my disciples if you love one another."

We have always concentrated more on the quality of the members themselves, which of course is vital. But our character is displayed in our relationships with each other; in the quality of the bonds we develop among ourselves. Jesus said His disciples would be known by their love for each other—by the depth of their relationships with each other! "By this, all men will know that you are my disciples, if you love one another."

The love and unity demonstrated within the church are powerful testimonies to the world. By prioritizing relationships and living out Christ's command to love one another, the church becomes a visible expression of God's love and grace.

Practical Application:

• Reflect on your current relationships within your church community. Consider how you can strengthen and nurture these connections to contribute to the unity and growth of the church.

• Commit to fostering an environment of love, support, and collaboration within your church, encouraging others to do the same.

Application

Ephesians 4:2-3 (NIV) - "Be completely humble and gentle; be patient, bearing with one another in love. Make every effort to keep the unity of the Spirit through the bond of peace."

Reflect on how you can contribute to the unity and strength of your church community, prioritizing relationships and fostering a spirit of love and collaboration. Consider how you can actively participate in building connections that support the growth and mission of the church.

Challenge Questions

1.   **In what ways can you actively contribute to strengthening relationships within your church, ensuring that each joint supplies and supports the growth of the body?** Reflect on your current involvement in your church community and consider how you can invest in building and nurturing relationships.

2.   **How can you cultivate a spirit of love and unity within your church, demonstrating the power of healthy relationships and connections?** Identify practical steps to foster an environment of support and collaboration, encouraging others to prioritize relationships and unity.

3.   **What steps can you take to ensure that your church community reflects the love and grace of Christ, becoming a visible expression of God's Kingdom?** Consider how you can contribute to creating a church community that is known for its love and unity, impacting the world with the message of the Gospel.

The strength and effectiveness of the church depend on the unity and health of its relationships. By prioritizing connections and fostering a spirit of love and collaboration, the church can thrive and fulfill its mission. Let us commit to building strong, healthy relationships that support the growth and impact of God's Kingdom.

Day 28
Just Attending Church

Hebrews 10:25 (NIV) "…Not forsaking the assembling of ourselves together, as is the manner of some, but exhorting one another, and so much the more as you see the Day approaching."

The Deeper Meaning of Assembling Together

Acts 2:42 (NIV) - "They devoted themselves to the apostles' teaching and to fellowship, to the breaking of bread and to prayer."

I was taught, as a young believer, that this scripture was God's wisdom to us that we should never forsake the discipline of attending church. This may generally be true, but it carries a more profound meaning and understanding than a mere act of attending a church meeting.

Attending church is more than just showing up; it involves actively participating in the community of believers. Assembling together is a process that requires transformation, organization, and augmentation. It means fitting together the various parts as one. That means placement is not to be taken lightly and must be taught as an essential component of a believer's purpose. Every believer must come to an understanding of his or her place in the body. This is taught but also must be caught by the believer. There must be a hunger to grasp this revelation.

Understanding Our Place in the Body

Ephesians 4:16 (NIV) - "From him, the whole body, joined and held together by every supporting ligament, grows and builds itself up in love, as each part does its work."

The Apostle Paul reminds us with the same instruction: "from whom the whole body, joined and knit together by what every joint supplies, according to the effective working by which every part does its share, causes growth of the body for the edifying of itself in love."

The church is not just a building; it is a living organism made up of diverse individuals, each with a unique role and purpose. Understanding our place in the body of Christ is crucial for the church to function effectively and fulfill its mission. Each member contributes to the overall health and growth of the community.

Beyond Mere Attendance

1 Corinthians 1:10 (NIV) - "I appeal to you, brothers and sisters, in the name of our Lord Jesus Christ, that all of you agree with one another in what you say and that there be no divisions among you, but that you be perfectly united in mind and thought."

Let's expound further... It is very possible for a local church to have all its members attend church and not come close to assembling themselves. Being in the same building does not signify being assembled. The goal is to be in the same place, same mind, same spirit, and same vision with the same values.

True assembly involves unity in purpose and alignment in vision. It requires intentionality in building relationships and working together toward common goals. When believers are united in heart and mind, the church becomes a powerful force for advancing God's Kingdom.

Creating a Culture of Assembly

Colossians 3:14-15 (NIV) - "And over all these virtues put on love, which binds them all together in perfect unity. Let the peace of Christ rule in your hearts, since as members of one body you were called to peace. And be thankful."

I know that my first goal is to just get people to attend, but my challenge has been creating a culture where the thought of not assembling cuts against the grain of their convictions and kingdom culture. I know one day we will be there; I just hope it's by choice and not by necessity.

Building a culture of assembly requires fostering an environment where relationships are prioritized, and community is valued. It involves encouraging one another to participate actively and contribute to the church's mission. As believers, we are called to support and uplift one another, creating a sense of belonging and purpose within the church.

Practical Application:

- Reflect on your current involvement in your church community. Consider how you can contribute to building a culture of assembly, where unity and purpose are prioritized.

- Commit to actively participating in church activities and building relationships with fellow believers, fostering a sense of community and belonging.

Application

Galatians 6:2 (NIV) - "Carry each other's burdens, and in this way, you will fulfill the law of Christ."

Reflect on how you can actively engage in your church community, prioritizing relationships and fostering a spirit of unity and collaboration. Consider how you can contribute to the overall health and growth of the church, supporting one another and working together toward common goals.

Challenge Questions

1.   **In what ways can you actively contribute to building a culture of assembly within your church, ensuring that relationships and unity are prioritized?** Reflect on your current involvement in your church community and consider how you can invest in building and nurturing relationships.

2.   **How can you cultivate a spirit of unity and collaboration within your church, demonstrating the power of assembling together as a community of believers?** Identify practical steps to foster an environment of support and collaboration, encouraging others to prioritize relationships and unity.

3.   **What steps can you take to ensure that your church community reflects the love and grace of Christ, becoming a visible expression of God's Kingdom?** Consider how you can contribute to creating a church community that is known for its love and unity, impacting the world with the message of the Gospel.

The effectiveness and impact of the church depend on the unity and health of its relationships. By prioritizing connections and fostering a spirit of love and collaboration, the church can thrive and fulfill its mission. Let us commit to building strong, healthy relationships that support the growth and impact of God's Kingdom.

Day 29

Do This in RE-MEMBERance of Me

Luke 22:19 (NIV) "And he took bread, gave thanks and broke it, and gave it to them, saying, 'This is my body given for you; do this in remembrance of me.'"

The Significance of Communion

1 Corinthians 11:23-26 (NIV) - "For I received from the Lord what I also passed on to you: The Lord Jesus, on the night he was betrayed, took bread, and when he had given thanks, he broke it and said, 'This is my body, which is for you; do this in remembrance of me.' In the same way, after supper, he took the cup, saying, 'This cup is the new covenant in my blood; do this, whenever you drink it, in remembrance of me.' For whenever you eat this bread and drink this cup, you proclaim the Lord's death until he comes."

There are various schools of thought about the Last Supper and communion. A part of Christianity believes in the literal meaning; that we must eat of His flesh and drink of His blood through a divine process called "transubstantiation." The rest believe that it was figurative; that by taking communion, we identify with His life and sacrifice for us on the cross.

The subject of communion is quite vast. To think that I will be able to explain it in a blog would be nonsensical, but let me point out one vantage point.

A Call for Unity and Remembrance

Ephesians 4:4-6 (NIV) - "There is one body and one Spirit, just as you were called to one hope when you were called; one Lord, one faith, one baptism; one God and Father of all, who is over all and through all and in all."

I believe it's more than the two schools of thought. It was a call for unity, agreement, and harmony. Jesus needed to create a sacrament that would require the church to remember. The bread and wine...the bread represented His body, which was broken and given to the disciples; the wine was shared and given to drink by every disciple. Both the bread and wine used to be whole, but when partaken, they became broken for us. He took the punishment—He became broken and dismembered so we wouldn't have to be.

The apostle Paul, in teaching the Corinthian church, said this: "...Now you are the body of Christ, and members individually" (1 Corinthians 12:27). We are the pieces that make up the body of Christ. We are all members of His body. In order for members to be functional, they cannot be alone; they must come together and operate in unison with each other. That is why Jesus said during the Last Passover meal and the first communion with His disciples, "...do this in 'Re-MEMBERance' of me." We are to RE-MEMBER the body. We have to bring it into physical being, as in the assembling of the parts of a puzzle into a whole. To "re-member" means to unite the body as a whole. This is why it's called communion—it means to have a common union.

Celebrating Unity in Communion

> **Colossians 3:14-15 (NIV)** - "And over all these virtues put on love, which binds them all together in perfect unity. Let the peace of Christ rule in your hearts, since as members of one body you were called to peace. And be thankful."

So the next time we celebrate at the table of the Lord, I would love for you to see it in this manner. It is a celebration of unity. That is why we cannot be in strife or discord with anyone, lest we partake of communion in contempt. Let's be one body—many members functioning together as one!

Communion is a powerful reminder of the unity we share as believers. It calls us to reflect on the sacrifice of Christ and the bond we have with one another through Him. By participating in communion with a heart of unity and love, we honor Christ and strengthen the bonds within the body of Christ.

Practical Application:

- Reflect on your relationships within the church community. Consider if there are any areas of discord or strife that need to be addressed before participating in communion.

- Commit to fostering unity and harmony within the body of Christ, recognizing that we are all members of one body, called to work together for God's Kingdom.

Application

Romans 12:5 (NIV) - "So in Christ, we, though many, form one body, and each member belongs to all the others."

Reflect on how you can actively contribute to the unity and strength of your church community, prioritizing relationships and fostering a spirit of love and collaboration. Consider how you can demonstrate the love and grace of Christ in your interactions with others.

Challenge Questions

1.   **In what ways can you actively contribute to building a culture of unity within your church, ensuring that relationships and harmony are prioritized?** Reflect on your current involvement in your church community and consider how you can invest in building and nurturing relationships.

2.   **How can you cultivate a spirit of love and collaboration within your church, demonstrating the power of communion as a celebration of unity?** Identify practical steps to foster an environment of support and collaboration, encouraging others to prioritize relationships and unity.

3.   **What steps can you take to ensure that your church community reflects the love and grace of Christ, becoming a visible expression of God's Kingdom?** Consider how you can contribute to creating a church community that is known for its love and unity, impacting the world with the message of the Gospel.

The significance of communion lies in its call for unity and remembrance. By participating in communion with a heart of love and collaboration, we honor Christ's sacrifice and strengthen the bonds within the body of Christ. Let us commit to building a strong, unified church community that reflects the love and grace of our Savior.

Day 30

Changing the Man in the Mirror

James 1:23-24 (NIV) "Anyone who listens to the word but does not do what it says is like someone who looks at his face in a mirror and, after looking at himself, goes away and immediately forgets what he looks like."

The Importance of Self-Knowledge

Proverbs 4:7 (NIV) - "The beginning of wisdom is this: Get wisdom. Though it cost all you have, get understanding."

Self-knowledge is the best kind of knowledge. The secret of knowledge is first having knowledge of yourself. We all have to make a personal commitment to grow spiritually, mentally, and socially. I heard someone once say, "You've got to do your own growing no matter how tall your Daddy is!"

Understanding who we are is the first step toward personal growth and transformation. By examining our thoughts, actions, and motivations, we gain insight into the areas where change is needed. This self-awareness is crucial for developing wisdom and making meaningful progress in our lives.

Reflecting on Personal Change

Romans 12:2 (NIV) - "Do not conform to the pattern of this world, but be transformed by the renewing of your mind. Then you will be able to test and approve what God's will is—his good, pleasing and perfect will."

I'm a History junkie, and when I visited Westminster Abbey in London, my mind was blown away by the different types of people buried there who were given the opportunity to change the world. Some did, and well… some just blew their chance. The following words were written on the tomb of an Anglican Bishop (1100 A.D.) in the Crypts of Westminster Abbey:

• When I was young and free and my imagination had no limits, I dreamed of changing the world. As I grew older and wiser, I discovered the world would not change, so I shortened my sights somewhat and decided to change only my country.

• But it, too, seemed immovable.

• As I grew into my twilight years, in one last desperate attempt, I settled for changing only my family, those closest to me, but alas, they would have none of it.

• *And now as I lie on my deathbed, I suddenly realized:* If I had changed myself first, then by example I would have changed my family. From their inspiration and encouragement, I would then have been able to better my country and, who knows, I may have even changed the world.

This poignant reflection highlights the importance of starting with personal change. Transforming ourselves can inspire those around us, creating a ripple effect that extends to our communities and beyond. True change begins with the individual, and through our actions and example, we can influence the world.

Overcoming Self as an Obstacle

Matthew 7:3-5 (NIV) - "Why do you look at the speck of sawdust in your brother's eye and pay no attention to the plank in your own eye? How can you say to your brother, 'Let me take the speck out of your eye,' when all the time there is a plank in your own eye? You hypocrite, first take the plank out of your own eye, and then you will see clearly to remove the speck from your brother's eye."

It all begins with the man in the mirror. We have to continue to fight the e-ne-me-in-a-me. We are our own enemy. We are our own obstacles to changing our world.

Often, the biggest barrier to personal growth is ourselves. Our fears, doubts, and insecurities can hinder our progress and prevent us from reaching our full potential. By recognizing and addressing these obstacles, we can begin the process of transformation and unlock our ability to impact the world around us.

Committing to Personal Growth

Philippians 3:12-14 (NIV) - "Not that I have already obtained all this, or have already arrived at my goal, but I press on to take hold of that for which Christ Jesus took hold of me. Brothers and sisters, I do not consider myself yet to have taken hold of it. But one thing I do: Forgetting what is behind and straining toward what is ahead, I press on toward the goal to win the prize for which God has called me heavenward in Christ Jesus."

Committing to personal growth involves a willingness to change, learn, and adapt. It requires humility and the desire to become the best version of ourselves. As we pursue growth, we become better equipped to fulfill our purpose and positively influence the world around us.

Practical Application:

- Reflect on your current state of self-knowledge. Identify areas where you may need to grow and change, and commit to pursuing personal transformation.

- Develop a plan for personal growth, setting specific goals and seeking accountability from trusted friends or mentors.

Application

2 Corinthians 3:18 (NIV) - "And we all, who with unveiled faces contemplate the Lord's glory, are being transformed into his image with ever-increasing glory, which comes from the Lord, who is the Spirit."

Reflect on how you can actively engage in personal growth and transformation, ensuring that your actions and decisions align with God's purposes. Consider how you can inspire others through your journey of change and become a positive influence in your community.

Challenge Questions

1. **In what areas of your life do you need to focus on personal growth and transformation, and how can you actively pursue change?** Reflect on your current state of self-knowledge and consider how you can develop a plan for personal growth.

2. **How can you overcome the obstacles that hinder your progress and prevent you from reaching your full potential?** Identify practical steps to address fears, doubts, and insecurities, allowing you to pursue personal growth and transformation.

3. **What steps can you take to inspire others through your journey of personal change, creating a positive impact in your community and beyond?** Consider how you can share your experiences and insights with others, encouraging them to embark on their journey of growth.

Personal growth and transformation are essential for fulfilling our God-given purpose and impacting the world around us. By focusing on self-knowledge and committing to change, we can become the best versions of ourselves and inspire others to do the same. Let us strive to overcome the obstacles within us and pursue growth with passion and determination.

Day 31
Keys to Connecting with Others

1 Thessalonians 2:8 (NIV) "So we cared for you. Because we loved you so much, we were delighted to share with you not only the gospel of God but our lives as well."

Initiate Movement Toward Them

Philippians 2:3-4 (NIV) - "Do nothing out of selfish ambition or vain conceit. Rather, in humility value others above yourselves, not looking to your own interests but each of you to the interests of the others."

Initiating movement toward others is the first step in building meaningful connections. It requires a willingness to step out of our comfort zones and engage with people on a personal level.

"The number one managerial productivity problem in America is, quite simply, managers who are out of touch with their people and out of touch with their customers." — Tom Peters & Nancy Austin

"There are many cases of salesmen who have nothing to offer a prospect except friendship out-selling salesmen with everything to offer — except friendship." — Charles B. Ruth

By taking the initiative to connect with others, we demonstrate genuine interest and care for their well-being. This proactive approach fosters trust and opens the door for deeper relationships.

Look for Common Ground

Romans 12:16 (NIV) - "Live in harmony with one another. Do not be proud but be willing to associate with people of low position. Do not be conceited."

Finding common ground is essential for building rapport and understanding with others. It involves actively listening and seeking to understand their perspectives, feelings, and experiences.

Four Words to Help You Meet Others on Emotional Common Ground:

- ***Feel:*** Try to sense what they feel and acknowledge and validate their feelings.
- ***Felt:*** Share with them that you have also felt the same way.
- ***Found:*** Share with them what you found that has helped you.
- ***Find:*** Offer to help them find help for their lives.

Finding common ground involves empathy and the ability to relate to others on a deeper level. By identifying shared experiences and emotions, we create a foundation for meaningful connections.

Find the Keys to People's Lives

To find the keys to a person's heart, ask these questions:

- What do you sing about?

- What do you cry about?

- What do you dream about?

These questions help uncover the deeper motivations and passions that drive people, allowing us to connect with them on a more personal and meaningful level.

Communicate from the Heart

> **Ephesians 4:29 (NIV)** - "Do not let any unwholesome talk come out of your mouths, but only what is helpful for building others up according to their needs, that it may benefit those who listen."

Once you've initiated a connection with others, found common ground, and discovered what really matters to them, communicate to them what really matters to you. And that requires you to speak to them from your heart.

- *Law of Connection:* Leaders touch a heart before they ask for a hand.

"If you would win a man to your cause, first convince him that you are his sincere friend." — Abraham Lincoln

Effective communication involves more than just words; it requires authenticity, sincerity, and a genuine desire to connect with others. By speaking from the heart, we build trust and foster deeper relationships.

Practical Application:

• Reflect on your current approach to connecting with others. Consider how you can take the initiative to engage with people on a personal level.

• Develop active listening skills and seek to understand the feelings and experiences of others, identifying common ground to build rapport.

Application

Colossians 3:12-14 (NIV) - "Therefore, as God's chosen people, holy and dearly loved, clothe yourselves with compassion, kindness, humility, gentleness, and patience. Bear with each other and forgive one another if any of you has a grievance against someone. Forgive as the Lord forgave you. And over all these virtues put on love, which binds them all together in perfect unity."

Reflect on how you can actively engage in building meaningful connections with others, prioritizing empathy, understanding, and communication from the heart. Consider how you can demonstrate the love and grace of Christ in your interactions with others.

Challenge Questions

1. **In what ways can you actively initiate connections with others, demonstrating genuine interest and care for their well-being?** Reflect on your current approach to building relationships and consider how you can take the initiative to engage with people on a personal level.

2. **How can you cultivate empathy and understanding, seeking common ground with others to build rapport and meaningful connections?** Identify practical steps to develop active listening skills and seek to understand the feelings and experiences of others.

3. **What steps can you take to communicate from the heart, building trust and fostering deeper relationships with those around you?** Consider how you can speak with authenticity and sincerity, demonstrating the love and grace of Christ in your interactions with others.

Building meaningful connections with others is essential for fulfilling our God-given purpose and impacting the world around us. By prioritizing empathy, understanding, and communication from the heart, we can develop deeper relationships and demonstrate the love and grace of Christ. Let us strive to connect with others in meaningful ways, creating a positive impact in our communities and beyond.

Day 32

His Light in Our Dark

Ephesians 1:18 (NIV) "I pray also that the eyes of your heart may be enlightened in order that you may know the hope to which he has called you…"

Navigating Dark and Uncertain Times

Psalm 27:1 (NIV) - "The Lord is my light and my salvation—whom shall I fear? The Lord is the stronghold of my life—of whom shall I be afraid?"

We all face dark and uncertain times in our lives. I believe there are daytimes and nighttimes in our journey of purpose with the Lord. The day times are times when things become clear and somewhat unproblematic in our journey. But the nighttimes are the contrary. In the nighttime season, the road becomes difficult to see. We slow our pace for fear that we take the wrong turn or maybe even collide with an obstacle. We must continue to pray the prayer that the apostle Paul prayed for us, "…that the eyes of your heart may be enlightened in order that you may know the hope to which he has called you…"

During dark times, it is essential to seek God's light to guide our path. The challenges and uncertainties we face can make it difficult to see the way forward, but God's presence provides the clarity and assurance we need to navigate through them.

The Power of Enlightenment

Psalm 119:105 (NIV) - "Your word is a lamp for my feet, a light on my path."

The word "enlightened" is the word photizo, meaning; make to see by allowing light in. It's the same concept as making a photograph. Light comes into a dark place and engraves the image it carries. This is what occurs when we allow God's revelation (Word) to illuminate our course. He gives to us a picture of our destiny. His reminds us to stay the course and not allow darkened distractions to detour us. His word is truly a, "lamp to our feet and a light to our path" (Ps. 119:105).

God's light reveals His purposes and plans for our lives, offering us hope and direction. By allowing His Word to illuminate our hearts and minds, we gain insight into His will and receive the strength to persevere through difficult times.

Staying the Course

John 8:12 (NIV) - *"When Jesus spoke again to the people, he said, 'I am the light of the world. Whoever follows me will never walk in darkness but will have the light of life.'"*

I'm not certain what you are going through right now, but I do know that I need His light more than ever. Darkness has a way of slowing down progress, but it also makes us walk more carefully as long as we walk in His light. I pray that you allow the Lord to enlighten your heart in order that you may know the hope to which he has called you.

In times of uncertainty, it is crucial to remain focused on God's promises and the hope we have in Him. By trusting in His guidance and staying committed to His path, we can overcome the challenges and obstacles we encounter.

Practical Application:

• Reflect on your current circumstances and identify areas where you need God's light and guidance. Spend time in prayer and seek His wisdom for your journey.

• Commit to reading and meditating on God's Word regularly, allowing it to illuminate your path and provide clarity and direction.

Application

2 Corinthians 4:6 (NIV) - "For God, who said, 'Let light shine out of darkness,' made his light shine in our hearts to give us the light of the knowledge of God's glory displayed in the face of Christ."

Reflect on how you can actively seek God's light during dark and uncertain times, ensuring that His Word and presence guide your path. Consider how you can stay focused on His promises and trust in His guidance, even when the way forward seems unclear.

Challenge Questions

1. **In what areas of your life do you need God's light and guidance to navigate through dark and uncertain times?** Reflect on your current circumstances and consider how you can seek His wisdom and direction for your journey.

2. **How can you allow God's Word to illuminate your path, providing clarity and direction during challenging times?** Identify practical steps to incorporate regular Bible study and meditation into your routine, allowing His light to guide you.

3. **What steps can you take to stay focused on God's promises and trust in His guidance, even when the way forward seems unclear?** Consider how you can remain committed to His path and trust in His plans, even in times of uncertainty.

Seeking God's light during dark and uncertain times is essential for navigating the challenges we face and fulfilling His purposes for our lives. By allowing His Word to illuminate our hearts and minds, we gain the clarity and direction we need to stay the course and trust in His promises. Let us commit to seeking His light and guidance, walking in faith and hope as we journey through life.

Day 33
Conditioned Reflex

Romans 8:1 (NIV) "Therefore, there is now no condemnation for those who are in Christ Jesus."

Understanding Conditioned Reflexes

Philippians 3:13-14 (NIV) - "Brothers and sisters, I do not consider myself yet to have taken hold of it. But one thing I do: Forgetting what is behind and straining toward what is ahead, I press on toward the goal to win the prize for which God has called me heavenward in Christ Jesus."

At the turn of the 20th century, a Russian psychologist named Ivan Pavlov won the Nobel Prize for studying the behavior of dogs. Dogs normally salivate at the sights and smell of food, but he wanted to see if he could cause salivation from other stimuli. As you may remember from school, he did this by ringing a bell every time he fed the dogs. Eventually, ringing the bell was enough in itself to cause salivation. Pavlov referred to this as a Conditioned Reflex.

Conditioned reflexes are learned responses to specific stimuli. They can be beneficial, such as developing a habit of checking your blind spot before changing lanes, but they can also be detrimental when they arise from negative experiences and limit our ability to move forward.

Recognizing Spiritual Conditioned Reflexes

1 John 3:20 (NIV) - "If our hearts condemn us, we know that God is greater than our hearts, and he knows everything."

When we sin, guilt is a healthy and holy conditioned reflex. This is caused by the conviction of the Holy Spirit; it drives and leads us to repentance. Conviction is a healthy conditioned reflex that is caused by God, but false guilt and condemnation are conditioned reflexes caused by the enemy that become like psychological straitjackets which immobilize us spiritually.

As leaders, every time we have a bad experience, we become conditioned to that experience, creating a reflex. I've been disappointed, backstabbed, lied about, falsely accused, and misrepresented, but I cannot allow these experiences to form a conditioned reflex that hinders my ability to lead. Likewise, I cannot be the source from where they come from. The ministry is a calling to a willingness to be attacked and injured and coupled with a compassion for the very people who do so.

Recognizing the difference between conviction and condemnation is crucial for our spiritual growth.

Conviction leads to positive change, while condemnation holds us back, preventing us from experiencing the fullness of God's grace and forgiveness.

Overcoming Negative Conditioned Reflexes

Hebrews 12:1 (NIV) - "Therefore, since we are surrounded by such a great cloud of witnesses, let us throw off everything that hinders and the sin that so easily entangles. And let us run with perseverance the race marked out for us."

My desire, as a leader and a senior pastor, is to create an environment where conditioned reflexes derive from good experiences, not bad ones. You see, conditioned reflexes from bad experiences cause us to be so fixated on our negative past that we fail to see our future opportunities. We even begin to think that our mistakes or our hurts will disqualify us from being used by God again. You cannot allow them to stop you.

It didn't stop the Apostle Peter... I bet you every time he heard a rooster crow, he had a conditioned reflex that reminded him of betraying Jesus. He had to hear one every morning! I'm sure he used it to continually remind himself of the grace and mercy of God. Don't let your failures define you; if Peter was able to push past it, so can we!

Overcoming negative conditioned reflexes requires a conscious effort to let go of past mistakes and focus on God's promises. By embracing His grace and forgiveness, we can move forward and fulfill our God-given purpose.

Practical Application:

• Reflect on any negative conditioned reflexes you may have developed from past experiences. Identify how they may be hindering your spiritual growth and seek God's guidance to overcome them.

• Focus on building positive conditioned reflexes by surrounding yourself with supportive, encouraging relationships and immersing yourself in God's Word.

Application

2 Corinthians 5:17 (NIV) - "Therefore, if anyone is in Christ, the new creation has come: The old has gone, the new is here!"

Reflect on how you can actively overcome negative conditioned reflexes and embrace the new creation you are in Christ. Consider how you can cultivate a mindset of grace and forgiveness, allowing you to move forward and fulfill your God-given purpose.

Challenge Questions

1. **In what areas of your life have negative conditioned reflexes developed, and how can you actively work to overcome them?** Reflect on your past experiences and consider how they may be influencing your present decisions and actions.

2. **How can you recognize the difference between conviction and condemnation in your spiritual journey, ensuring that you respond to God's guidance with grace and humility?** Identify practical steps to discern between these two influences and seek God's wisdom in responding appropriately.

3. **What steps can you take to build positive conditioned reflexes, creating an environment that supports your spiritual growth and development?** Consider how you can surround yourself with supportive relationships and immerse yourself in God's Word to foster positive change.

Understanding and overcoming conditioned reflexes is essential for spiritual growth and fulfilling our God-given purpose. By recognizing the difference between conviction and condemnation and focusing on God's grace and forgiveness, we can move forward and embrace the new creation we are in Christ. Let us strive to cultivate positive conditioned reflexes and live lives that reflect His love and grace.

Day 34

Thoughts on Goal Setting

Proverbs 16:3 (NIV) "Commit to the Lord whatever you do, and he will establish your plans."

Understanding the Frustration with Goal Setting

Philippians 3:13-14 (NIV) - "Brothers and sisters, I do not consider myself yet to have taken hold of it. But one thing I do: Forgetting what is behind and straining toward what is ahead, I press on toward the goal to win the prize for which God has called me heavenward in Christ Jesus."

Have you ever been frustrated with goal setting? Have you ever had anyone inspire you to set goals? Let me guess, you shot for the moon but only hit the top of the tree line?! Don't worry, you're not the only one guilty of this, it's been my frustration also. There was one year that I didn't set any goals at all; what I did was adopt the previous year's goals, cut them in half, to feel good about accomplishing something! I realized my problem…I needed to set goals that were difficult yet still attainable. I needed to remove my ego and ambition out of the way and allow the Lord to lead me and push me into fruitfulness.

Setting realistic and achievable goals is essential for maintaining motivation and progress. By aligning our goals with God's guidance and purpose for our lives, we can experience fulfillment and growth in our journey.

Key Principles of Goal Setting

Proverbs 21:5 (NIV) - "The plans of the diligent lead to profit as surely as haste leads to poverty."

Here are a few thoughts about goals and goal setting:

• *Clear, Measurable, and Time-Bound:* Goals need to be clear, measurable, and time-bound. Many people think they have goals, but in reality, what they have is a series of wishes and wants. Clear goals provide a roadmap for success and help us stay focused on what truly matters.

• *Direction and Purpose:* Goals give us a sense of direction and purpose. I heard someone say, "If you don't know where you are going, then any road will take you there." Goals help us stay on track and ensure that our efforts align with our ultimate objectives.

• *Unlocking Potential and Creativity:* Goals unlock our potential and release creativity. Your potential and creativity are always birthed from a desire to accomplish a goal. By setting challenging goals, we push ourselves to think outside the box and discover new solutions.

• ***Enthusiasm and Vision:*** Goals give us enthusiasm and power to live fully in the present but with vision and foresight of our future. They help us see the big picture and inspire us to take meaningful action toward our dreams.

• ***Clarity and Efficiency:*** Goals give us clarity and help us operate more efficiently. They become the measuring rod for success by increasing performance and removing needless conflict and duplication of effort (boy, have I been guilty of this!).

Staying Committed to Your Goals

Habakkuk 2:2 (NIV) - "Then the Lord replied: 'Write down the revelation and make it plain on tablets so that a herald may run with it.'"

If you have already set goals for the year but have wandered away from them, revisit them and stay the course. Now, if you sense you have to adjust them in order to obtain a victory, please do so – it will be very encouraging! I recently adjusted the goals for our church and our leadership team. Passion, Unity, and Consistency have been our keys to building the momentum we are currently in. I am fully confident we will obtain our goals – I just know it!!

Staying committed to your goals requires perseverance and flexibility. By revisiting and adjusting your goals as needed, you can maintain momentum and ensure that your efforts align with God's purpose for your life.

Practical Application:

• Reflect on your current goals and assess whether they are clear, measurable, and aligned with God's purpose for your life. Make any necessary adjustments to ensure they are realistic and achievable.

• Develop a plan for staying committed to your goals, incorporating regular reviews and accountability measures to track your progress and make adjustments as needed.

Application

James 1:5 (NIV) - "If any of you lacks wisdom, you should ask God, who gives generously to all without finding fault, and it will be given to you."

Reflect on how you can actively set and pursue goals that align with God's purpose for your life. Consider how you can stay committed to your goals and seek God's guidance and wisdom as you strive to achieve them.

Challenge Questions

1.   **In what areas of your life do you need to set or adjust goals to ensure they are clear, measurable, and aligned with God's purpose?** Reflect on your current goals and consider how you can make any necessary adjustments to ensure they are realistic and achievable.

2.   **How can you stay committed to your goals and maintain momentum, even when faced with challenges and setbacks?** Identify practical steps to incorporate regular reviews and accountability measures to track your progress and make adjustments as needed.

3.   **What steps can you take to ensure that your goals unlock your potential and creativity, allowing you to live with enthusiasm and vision for the future?** Consider how you can set challenging goals that inspire you to think outside the box and discover new solutions.

Setting and pursuing meaningful goals is essential for fulfilling our God-given purpose and living with intention and clarity. By aligning our goals with God's guidance and purpose for our lives, we can experience fulfillment and growth in our journey. Let us strive to set clear, measurable, and achievable goals, staying committed to our path and trusting in God's wisdom and guidance.

Day 35

Diligence with Goals

Proverbs 12:24 (NIV) "Diligent hands will rule, but laziness ends in slave labor."

Proverbs 6:10-11 (NIV) "A little sleep, a little slumber, a little folding of the hands to rest— and poverty will come on you like a bandit and scarcity like an armed man."

The Importance of Diligence

Colossians 3:23 (NIV) - "Whatever you do, work at it with all your heart, as working for the Lord, not for human masters."

We were designed to work. We were proposed to undertake tasks and to finish them. Our purpose and destiny will never be obtained and carried out until we develop a work ethic. A work ethic is simply a discipline, dedication, and a belief in the moral value of hard work. Work is diligence; and diligence is a virtue that every believer in Christ must possess in order to be found fruitful. But on the contrary, laziness is a vice, that if embraced by the believer, it will render them useless to the kingdom of God.

Diligence is a key component of a successful and purposeful life. It involves consistent effort, dedication, and a commitment to excellence in all that we do. By cultivating diligence, we align ourselves with God's purpose and position ourselves for success in achieving our goals.

The Role of Goals in Diligence

Proverbs 21:5 (NIV) - "The plans of the diligent lead to profit as surely as haste leads to poverty."

Goals to the diligent promote a strong organizational life. Being diligent without goals is business without productivity. Goals help us evaluate our progress. It's not how much we do (activity and business) that counts, rather the actual progress we make.

Here are some insights into what I've learned about goals throughout the years:

• ***Meaningful and Challenging:*** Your goals must be meaningful and challenging. They must be something you really want. Meaningful goals inspire us to push beyond our limits and strive for greatness.

• ***Aligned with Values:*** Your goals must line up with your personal values and what's important to you. Goals that align with our values keep us motivated and focused on what truly matters.

• ***Sacrifice and Commitment:*** What are you prepared to give up in order to achieve your goals? Achieving goals will always cost you something! The willingness to sacrifice and commit is essential for success.

• ***Specific and Measurable:*** Your goals must be specific and measurable. Clear goals provide a roadmap for success and allow us to track our progress.

• *Achievable and Realistic:* Your goals must be achievable. Don't overestimate and don't underestimate either. Make them difficult yet achievable. Realistic goals challenge us without overwhelming us.

• *Flexible:* Your goals must be flexible. Flexibility allows you to regulate and tweak your goals without abandoning them. Being open to adjustments ensures we stay on track despite changing circumstances.

Embracing Diligence in Goal Setting

Hebrews 12:11 (NIV) - "No discipline seems pleasant at the time, but painful. Later on, however, it produces a harvest of righteousness and peace for those who have been trained by it."

With this in mind, embrace the goals set before you, whether personal or corporate. They will organize and structure your life in such a way you've never thought of before. Let's stay focused and diligent, and let's achieve the goals set before us.

Diligence requires discipline and perseverance. By embracing these qualities and setting meaningful goals, we position ourselves for success and fulfillment in all areas of life.

Practical Application:

• Reflect on your current goals and assess whether they align with your values and priorities. Make any necessary adjustments to ensure they are meaningful and challenging.

• Develop a plan for maintaining diligence in your pursuit of goals, incorporating regular reviews and accountability measures to track your progress.

Application

Galatians 6:9 (NIV) - "Let us not become weary in doing good, for at the proper time we will reap a harvest if we do not give up."

Reflect on how you can actively cultivate diligence in your pursuit of goals, ensuring that your efforts align with God's purpose for your life. Consider how you can maintain focus and perseverance, even when faced with challenges and setbacks.

Challenge Questions

1. **In what areas of your life do you need to cultivate diligence and set meaningful goals that align
with your values and priorities?** Reflect on your current goals and consider how you can make any necessary
adjustments to ensure they are meaningful and challenging.

2. **How can you maintain diligence and perseverance in your pursuit of goals, even when faced
with challenges and setbacks?** Identify practical steps
to incorporate regular reviews and accountability measures
to track your progress and make adjustments as needed.

3. **What steps can you take to ensure that your
goals are specific, measurable, achievable, and
flexible, allowing you to stay on track and achieve
success?** Consider how you can set realistic goals that
inspire you to push beyond your limits and strive for greatness.

Diligence in setting and pursuing goals is essential for fulfilling our God-given
purpose and living with intention and clarity. By aligning our goals with God's
guidance and purpose for our lives, we can experience fulfillment and growth
in our journey. Let us strive to cultivate diligence and perseverance, staying
focused on our path and trusting in God's wisdom and guidance.

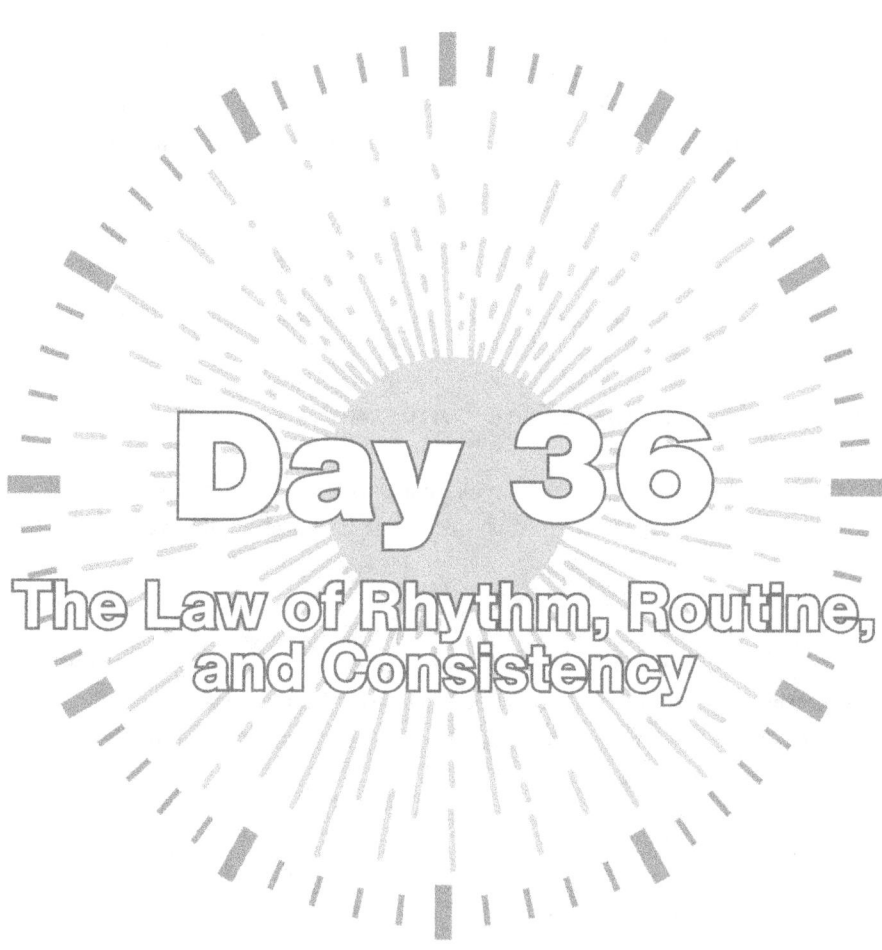

Day 36
The Law of Rhythm, Routine, and Consistency

1 Corinthians 16:1-2 (NIV) "Now about the collection for the Lord's people: Do what I told the Galatian churches to do. On the first day of every week, each one of you should set aside a sum of money in keeping with your income, saving it up, so that when I come no collections will have to be made."

The Power of Consistency

Galatians 6:9 (NIV) - "Let us not become weary in doing good, for at the proper time we will reap a harvest if we do not give up."

There is always evidence of results in consistency. Anything that you practice continuously will produce in and for you on a consistent and continuous basis. In the Kingdom of God, when it comes to finances, an erratic and irregular behavior in sowing seeds of tithing and offering will only bring you to times of lack and insufficiency. Our giving must become a routine and a pattern in order for us to see the results of it.

Consistency is key to success in any area of life. By developing a routine and sticking to it, we create an environment for growth and progress. Consistent actions lead to consistent results, whether in our spiritual lives, finances, or personal development.

Obeying the Laws of the Universe

Genesis 8:22 (NIV) - "As long as the earth endures, seedtime and harvest, cold and heat, summer and winter, day and night will never cease."

These results come from obeying laws. Laws are rules of operation in the universe, placed by God, that if obeyed and followed, will bring increase and success to us. Science tells us that the landing of a rocket on the moon is equivalent to shooting a mosquito with a rifle six miles away. You may ask, "how do they do it then?" It's by simply obeying the laws of the universe and math.

Learning the power of rhythm, routine, and consistency in sowing and reaping will lead us to a place of continual supply and increase. We must partner with the laws and principles of the Kingdom of God. Failure to do so will result in a failure to experience God's provision in our lives.

God's laws govern the universe and provide a framework for success and productivity. By aligning ourselves with these laws and principles, we position ourselves for spiritual and material growth.

Embracing Rhythm, Routine, and Consistency

Proverbs 3:9-10 (NIV) - "Honor the Lord with your wealth, with the firstfruits of all your crops; then your barns will be filled to overflowing, and your vats will brim over with new wine."

The following might sound very simplistic, but if followed through, it will produce a harvest of increase in our lives. The Apostle Paul said, "Now about the collection for God's people: Do what I told the Galatian churches to do. On the first day of every week, each one of you should set aside a sum of money in keeping with his income, saving it up, so that when I come no collections will have to be made." Routine, discipline, consistency, and rhythm; we can't quit on them.

Understand that reaping does not follow sowing – but waiting follows sowing. We sow, we wait, and we reap! In order to experience a continuous harvest of resources, there must be a continuous sowing of seeds to accommodate the seasons of waiting. Remember Genesis 8:22, "As long as the earth endures, seedtime and harvest, cold and heat, summer and winter, day and night will never cease." They are consistent laws of the universe that must be obeyed in order to live a life of productivity. Let's remain consistent to the laws of the Kingdom!

By embracing rhythm, routine, and consistency, we create a foundation for success and growth. These principles allow us to navigate the seasons of waiting and trust in God's provision for our lives.

Practical Application:

- Reflect on your current routines and practices, identifying areas where you can improve consistency and align with God's principles.

- Develop a plan for maintaining rhythm and routine in your spiritual and personal life, incorporating regular reviews and accountability measures to track your progress.

Application

Matthew 25:21 (NIV) - "His master replied, 'Well done, good and faithful servant! You have been faithful with a few things; I will put you in charge of many things. Come and share your master's happiness!'"

Reflect on how you can actively embrace rhythm, routine, and consistency in your spiritual and personal life, ensuring that your actions align with God's principles and laws. Consider how you can maintain diligence and perseverance in your pursuit of growth and productivity.

Challenge Questions

1.   **In what areas of your life do you need to cultivate consistency and align with God's principles and laws for growth and productivity?** Reflect on your current routines and practices, identifying areas where you can improve consistency and align with God's principles.

2.   **How can you maintain rhythm and routine in your spiritual and personal life, ensuring that you stay on track and experience God's provision?** Identify practical steps to incorporate regular reviews and accountability measures to track your progress and make adjustments as needed.

3.   **What steps can you take to ensure that you remain diligent and faithful in your pursuit of growth and productivity, trusting in God's provision and guidance?** Consider how you can develop a plan for maintaining rhythm and routine in your life, allowing you to navigate seasons of waiting and trust in God's provision.

Embracing the law of rhythm, routine, and consistency is essential for spiritual and material growth. By aligning our actions with God's principles and laws, we position ourselves for success and productivity. Let us strive to cultivate consistency and perseverance, staying focused on our path and trusting in God's provision and guidance.

Day 37

What You Don't Know Can and Will Hurt You!

2 Peter 1:3 (NIV) "His divine power has given us everything we need for life and godliness through our knowledge of him who called us by his own glory and goodness."

The Importance of Knowledge and Understanding

Proverbs 4:7 (NIV) - "The beginning of wisdom is this: Get wisdom. Though it cost all you have, get understanding."

I grew up hearing from various people the concept "whatever you don't know can't hurt you." That has got to be the most obtuse and brainless statement I have ever heard! It doesn't apply to anything in life except the possibility of being charged as an accomplice with an unlawful offense (although being involved in the situation carries a form of stupidity within it). In this case, not knowing information might not incriminate you. But other than that, I can't think of another reason why that statement is supposed to have any kind of sensible truthfulness to it at all.

Knowledge, understanding, and insight are all facets of wisdom. Knowledge is the foundation of everything. The Holy Spirit gave Peter an astonishing truth in 2 Peter 1:3. God's power has already given us everything we need to live our lives in righteousness and in total prosperity. But the only way we can tap into that power of provision is in "knowing Jesus." There are only two ways to increase our knowledge of Christ in our lives: through prayer and reading His Book. These two components, when done with understanding and passion, will elevate us to a greater platform of receptivity from God!

The Power of Knowing Christ

Philippians 3:10 (NIV) - "I want to know Christ—yes, to know the power of his resurrection and participation in his sufferings, becoming like him in his death."

The word knowledge is the Greek word epignōsis. Its root word is epiginōskō, which means to become thoroughly acquainted with, to know thoroughly, to know accurately, and to know well. It also means to recognize by hearing—to perceive whom a person is. So, in this case, to say "WHAT YOU DON'T KNOW CAN'T HURT YOU" is asinine in its full context! People, let's not be unintelligent and boorish when it comes to intimately knowing God, and let's not be ignorant and illiterate when it comes to His Word. WHO and WHAT you don't know will give you serious damage!

Knowing Christ is more than just acquiring information; it is about developing a deep, personal relationship with Him. This knowledge empowers us to live lives of purpose, strength, and fulfillment, equipped with everything we need to navigate the challenges of life.

Growing in Knowledge and Wisdom

Colossians 1:9-10 (NIV) - "For this reason, since the day we heard about you, we have not stopped praying for you. We continually ask God to fill you with the knowledge of his will through all the wisdom and understanding that the Spirit gives, so that you may live a life worthy of the Lord and please him in every way: bearing fruit in every good work, growing in the knowledge of God."

To grow in knowledge and wisdom, we must be intentional in our pursuit of understanding. This involves dedicating time to prayer and studying God's Word, allowing His truth to shape our thoughts, actions, and decisions.

By seeking wisdom and understanding, we position ourselves to receive God's blessings and guidance, enabling us to live lives that reflect His glory and purpose.

Practical Application:

• Commit to a regular routine of prayer and Bible study, seeking to grow in your knowledge and understanding of Christ.

• Surround yourself with a community of believers who encourage and challenge you to deepen your relationship with God.

Application

James 1:5 (NIV) - "If any of you lacks wisdom, you should ask God, who gives generously to all without finding fault, and it will be given to you."

Reflect on how you can actively pursue knowledge and understanding, ensuring that your life is guided by the wisdom and truth found in Christ. Consider how you can deepen your relationship with Him through prayer and study of His Word.

Challenge Questions

1.   **In what areas of your life do you need to grow in knowledge and understanding, ensuring that you are equipped to navigate challenges and opportunities?** Reflect on your current level of understanding and identify areas where you can deepen your knowledge and relationship with Christ.

2.   **How can you develop a routine of prayer and Bible study that allows you to grow in your knowledge and understanding of God's will for your life?** Identify practical steps to incorporate regular prayer and study into your daily routine, seeking God's wisdom and guidance.

3.   **What steps can you take to ensure that you are continually growing in your relationship with Christ, allowing His truth to shape your thoughts, actions, and decisions?** Consider how you can engage with a community of believers who encourage and challenge you to deepen your relationship with God.

Pursuing knowledge and understanding is essential for spiritual growth and fulfilling God's purpose for our lives. By seeking wisdom and developing a deep, personal relationship with Christ, we position ourselves to receive His guidance and blessings. Let us strive to grow in our knowledge and understanding, ensuring that our lives are guided by His truth and wisdom.

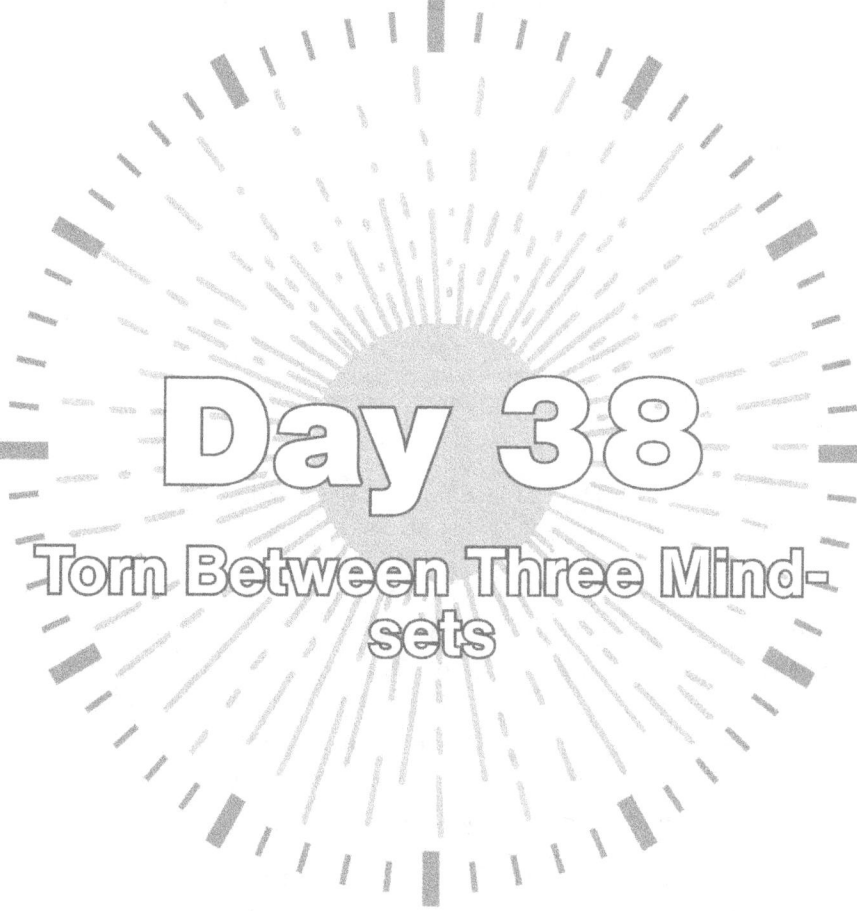

Day 38

Torn Between Three Mind-sets

Proverbs 27:12 (NIV) "The prudent see danger and take refuge, but the simple keep going and suffer for it."

Understanding the Three Mindsets

Proverbs 19:20 (NIV) - "Listen to advice and accept discipline, and at the end you will be counted among the wise."

When it comes to decision-making, I've seen three different types of mindsets in operation since since being born-again. There is the mindset of the simple (naïve), the prudent, and the ultra-prudent. We all know that our tenure here on earth is simply a journey. And within this journey, we make decisions that arrive at certain destinations. By the way, as long as you are living, a destination is not a final arriving point but rather a current point of arrival caused by past decisions. So, in case you've made some really bad decisions, like myself, there is always time to make some good ones, thus altering your current destination.

Understanding these mindsets can help us navigate the journey of life more effectively, ensuring that our decisions lead to desirable destinations and align with God's will.

The Simple Mindset

Proverbs 14:15 (NIV) - "The simple believe anything, but the prudent give thought to their steps."

Let me write about myself, and within these words, let me know where you're located... My struggle is in training myself to be prudent. I've been a risk-taker all my life. As a matter of fact, when I don't take risks, I get quite bored. That has its advantages and disadvantages. Unfortunately, I have suffered from bad decisions caused by risk-taking, thus bringing me to certain undesired destinations. According to the scripture above, when I take uncalculated and inconsiderate risks, I am taking the way of the simple – the naive.

The simple mindset often leads to impulsive decisions without considering potential consequences. This mindset lacks foresight and wisdom, resulting in undesired outcomes and missed opportunities.

The Ultra-Prudent Mindset

Ecclesiastes 11:4 (NIV) - "Whoever watches the wind will not plant; whoever looks at the clouds will not reap."

On the other hand – honestly speaking – I would rather be proactive (ok…simple-minded) than ultra-prudent. The ultra-prudent never move or take too long in decision-making. They discuss what they want to do and where they want to go, but their indecision negotiates them out of it. In reality, negative filters and ultimately fear cause this type of wavering. Hey, I would rather try something than not try anything at all! I'm just sayin….

The ultra-prudent mindset is characterized by excessive caution and indecision. Fear and over-analysis can prevent action, leading to missed opportunities and stagnation. Balancing caution with boldness is essential for effective decision-making.

The Prudent Mindset

Proverbs 8:12 (NIV) - "I, wisdom, dwell together with prudence; I possess knowledge and discretion."

The secret is in being PRUDENT. Being prudent is knowing how to be wise, discreet, and cautious, yet courageous, audacious, and bold. It's a delicate balance between being simple and ultra-prudent. The difference between the prudent and the ultra-prudent is that the prudent actually pulls the trigger. They make decisions in the face of their concerns. And the difference between the prudent and the simple is the reason for this blog… it's foresight. Learning to be prudent is seeing the big picture, thus learning not to fall into ruts and traps. Prudent people know that all life is connected and every decision will take you to a desired or undesired destination.

The prudent mindset embraces wisdom and foresight, enabling us to make informed decisions that align with our values and goals. By seeking God's guidance and considering potential outcomes, we can navigate life's journey with confidence and purpose.

Practical Application:

- Reflect on your current decision-making style and identify areas where you can cultivate prudence and foresight.

- Seek God's guidance and wisdom in your decision-making process, incorporating prayer and discernment to align your choices with His will.

Application

James 1:5 (NIV) - "If any of you lacks wisdom, you should ask God, who gives generously to all without finding fault, and it will be given to you."

Reflect on how you can actively cultivate a prudent mindset, ensuring that your decisions align with God's will and lead to desirable outcomes. Consider how you can balance caution with boldness, embracing wisdom and foresight in your journey.

Challenge Questions

1. **In what areas of your life do you need to cultivate prudence and foresight, ensuring that your decisions align with God's will and lead to desirable outcomes?** Reflect on your current decision-making style and identify areas where you can improve your ability to make informed and wise choices.

2. **How can you balance caution with boldness in your decision-making process, ensuring that you take action while considering potential consequences?** Identify practical steps to incorporate wisdom and foresight into your decision-making, seeking God's guidance and wisdom.

3. **What steps can you take to ensure that your decisions are guided by God's wisdom and understanding, allowing you to navigate life's journey with confidence and purpose?** Consider how you can develop a routine of prayer and discernment, seeking God's guidance in all aspects of your life.

Cultivating a prudent mindset is essential for effective decision-making and fulfilling God's purpose for our lives. By seeking wisdom and foresight, we can navigate life's journey with confidence and purpose, ensuring that our decisions align with God's will and lead to desirable outcomes. Let us strive to embrace prudence in our decision-making, balancing caution with boldness and trusting in God's guidance and wisdom.

Day 39

Prodigality

Luke 15:22-24 (NIV) "But the father said to his servants, 'Quick! Bring the best robe and put it on him. Put a ring on his finger and sandals on his feet. Bring the fattened calf and kill it. Let's have a feast and celebrate. For this son of mine was dead and is alive again; he was lost and is found.' So they began to celebrate."

Understanding Prodigality

1 John 3:1 (NIV) - "See what great love the Father has lavished on us, that we should be called children of God! And that is what we are!"

Words, at times, inherit connotations and undertones when used in certain notable situations. Certain words are used in famous stories, therefore adopting these undertones that associate them with the story. For example, when we hear the story of the Prodigal Son in Luke 15, we immediately think that it's a story of a "son gone wild." We get this implication that the word prodigal has to do with backsliding. After all, he left his father's home, then later repented and came back. The father received him and threw a party for him. Great parable, but understand something here... the word prodigal has nothing to do with being bitter toward God in a backslidden, non-repented attitude. Rather, it means being recklessly extravagant, characterized by lavish expenditure, being plenteous, yielding abundantly, luxuriant, or profuse in spending resources. In reality, being prodigal is neither good nor bad. Now if you read the story carefully, the father (who represents God) was also a prodigal. Hmm... I'll explain later...

Being a prodigal means being extravagant and seemingly wasteful. We are guilty of prodigality in many areas of our lives. We disconnect ourselves from the house of God and live our lives for ourselves. I recently received an email from an individual who hasn't been at church for several weeks now. In this email, this person justified himself by saying he hadn't been "sinning" but that he just needed his own space. The very thing the "prodigal son" wanted...his own space to do whatever he wanted to do. The fact of the matter is that our lives are not our own. We have been bought with a price...we exist to serve a divine purpose. Every waking moment that we don't, we are being prodigals.

Positive Prodigality

2 Corinthians 9:8 (NIV) - "And God is able to bless you abundantly, so that in all things at all times, having all that you need, you will abound in every good work."

On the other hand, prodigality is not bad when it's used positively. I want to be a prodigal when it comes to serving God. My prayer is that my children become prodigals with their lives for the cause of Christ. I want to lavishly spend my life training leaders and connecting people to the kingdom of God. After all, was not the father in the story a prodigal himself? When the son returned home, he immediately began to spend and give away resources. He threw such a huge party that the older brother became jealous and surely thought to himself that all of this was a waste! I believe God becomes a prodigal every time we come to our senses and connect ourselves back to the purpose he called us to. He wants us to be prodigals for the sake of his kingdom! "How great is the love the Father has lavished on us, that we should be called children of God! And that is what we are!" (**1 John 3:1**)

Embracing positive prodigality means being willing to invest our time, resources, and energy into the kingdom of God, knowing that our efforts will yield abundant fruit and blessings.

Practical Application:

- Reflect on areas of your life where you may be exhibiting negative prodigality, and consider how you can redirect your focus and resources toward serving God's purposes.

- Embrace a mindset of positive prodigality by finding ways to lavishly serve God and others, using your gifts and talents for His glory.

Application

Matthew 6:20-21 (NIV) - "But store up for yourselves treasures in heaven, where moths and vermin do not destroy, and where thieves do not break in and steal. For where your treasure is, there your heart will be also."

Reflect on how you can actively embrace positive prodigality, ensuring that your resources and efforts are directed toward serving God and building His kingdom. Consider how you can cultivate a mindset of abundance and generosity, allowing God's love to flow through you.

Challenge Questions

1. **In what areas of your life do you need to redirect your focus and resources toward serving God's purposes, ensuring that you are not exhibiting negative prodigality?** Reflect on your current habits and priorities, identifying areas where you can cultivate a mindset of positive prodigality.

2. **How can you embrace a mindset of positive prodigality, using your gifts and talents to serve God and others with abundance and generosity?** Identify practical steps to invest your time, resources, and energy into the kingdom of God, knowing that your efforts will yield abundant fruit and blessings.

3. **What steps can you take to ensure that your resources and efforts are directed toward serving God and building His kingdom, allowing His love to flow through you?** Consider how you can cultivate a mindset of abundance and generosity, embracing positive prodigality in your journey of faith.

Embracing positive prodigality is essential for fulfilling God's purpose and living a life of abundance and generosity. By redirecting our focus and resources toward serving God and building His kingdom, we position ourselves to receive His blessings and make a lasting impact. Let us strive to embrace positive prodigality, ensuring that our efforts reflect God's love and purpose in all we do.

Day 40

It's as Simple as Hearing and Doing

James 1:22 (NIV) "Do not merely listen to the word, and so deceive yourselves. Do what it says."

Embracing Simplicity

Matthew 7:24 (NIV) - "Therefore everyone who hears these words of mine and puts them into practice is like a wise man who built his house on the rock."

Most of us are great at complicating things. For whatever reason, we love to set hurdles for ourselves and confuse what would appear to be simplistic. I don't know why, at times, we seem to major in minors. It's always easier to recognize this in other people meanwhile remaining sightless to our own situations. I think I'm entering a season where I'm beginning to learn how to keep things simple. I'm learning that the profound is always discovered in the minimal. At every crossroads and decision in life, embracing the simple principles of God's word will cause us to stay on the path of purpose designed for us.

Simplicity is often overlooked, yet it holds profound power in our spiritual journey. By focusing on the basics of hearing and doing God's Word, we can navigate life's challenges with clarity and purpose.

Hearing the Word of God

Romans 10:17 (NIV) - "Consequently, faith comes from hearing the message, and the message is heard through the word about Christ."

When making decisions, understand that our "doing" cannot be disconnected from our "hearing." The boundaries or the limit of our lives are determined by His Word and not by our abilities or inabilities. Hearing and understanding are necessities.

In hearing, it's in our cooperation that produces a manifestation of God's initiation. Though prudency is essential, when overemphasized, it can become a hindrance in moving forcefully into what God has already spoken. Once the word is heard, action is required.

Hearing God's Word is the foundation of our faith and understanding. It requires attentiveness and receptivity, allowing His truth to guide our thoughts, actions, and decisions.

Doing the Word of God

Luke 11:28 (NIV) - "He replied, 'Blessed rather are those who hear the word of God and obey it.'"

Move beyond the fear of failure. Fear produces three types of fruit – paralysis, procrastination, and purposelessness. Doing the Word is the greatest example of submission to God. Doing the Word will require the death of our own will and the embracing of His will.

Action is a natural extension of hearing. By putting God's Word into practice, we demonstrate our faith and commitment to His will, overcoming fear and doubt with courage and obedience.

Practical Application:

• Reflect on areas of your life where you may be complicating your faith, and consider how you can simplify your approach by focusing on hearing and doing God's Word.

• Develop a routine of listening to and studying God's Word, allowing it to guide your actions and decisions with clarity and purpose.

Application

Philippians 4:9 (NIV) - "Whatever you have learned or received or heard from me, or seen in me—put it into practice. And the God of peace will be with you."

Reflect on how you can actively embrace simplicity in your faith, ensuring that your life is guided by the basics of hearing and doing God's Word. Consider how you can overcome fear and doubt by focusing on obedience and action.

Challenge Questions

1.   **In what areas of your life do you need to simplify your approach, ensuring that you focus on hearing and doing God's Word with clarity and purpose?** Reflect on your current habits and priorities, identifying areas where you can simplify your approach to faith and obedience.

2.   **How can you develop a routine of listening to and studying God's Word, allowing it to guide your actions and decisions with clarity and purpose?** Identify practical steps to incorporate regular listening and study into your daily routine, seeking God's guidance and wisdom.

3.   **What steps can you take to overcome fear and doubt, ensuring that your life is guided by the basics of hearing and doing God's Word with courage and obedience?** Consider how you can cultivate a mindset of simplicity and action, allowing God's truth to shape your thoughts, actions, and decisions.

Embracing simplicity in faith is essential for fulfilling God's purpose and living with clarity and purpose. By focusing on the basics of hearing and doing God's Word, we position ourselves to navigate life's challenges with confidence and obedience. Let us strive to embrace simplicity, ensuring that our actions reflect God's love and purpose in all we do.

Reflections on the Journey

As we reach the culmination of our 40-day journey of transformation, it is a time to reflect on the profound changes we have experienced and the truths we have discovered along the way. This journey has been one of deep spiritual renewal, where we have allowed God to work within us, reshaping our hearts and minds to reflect His love and grace.

The number 40 has guided us through a sacred period of growth and preparation, echoing the biblical journeys of transformation that marked pivotal moments in the lives of God's people. From the Israelites' 40 years in the wilderness to Jesus' 40 days of fasting and prayer, we have walked a path of testing, perseverance, and revelation. Through this, we have learned that transformation is not a destination but a lifelong journey of becoming more like Christ.

In this journey, we have discovered the importance of **endurance**. Hebrews 12:1 encourages us to "run with perseverance the race marked out for us." We have faced challenges and trials, yet we have also witnessed the strength that comes from leaning on God's promises and trusting in His unfailing love. Our trials have not been in vain; they have been the crucible through which our faith has been refined.

We have also experienced the power of **community**. Ecclesiastes 4:9-10 reminds us, "Two are better than one... if either of them falls, the one will lift up his companion." In our journey, we have learned that transformation is both personal and communal. We are called to support and uplift one another, recognizing that we are stronger together. Our growth is intertwined with the growth of those around us, and together we create a tapestry of faith that reflects God's kingdom on earth.

Forgiveness has been another key theme of our journey. We have explored the liberating power of forgiving others and ourselves, recognizing that forgiveness is not just an act but a transformation of the heart. As Ephesians 4:32 instructs, "Be kind and compassionate to one another, forgiving each other, just as in Christ God forgave you." In forgiveness, we find healing and freedom, allowing us to step into the future unburdened by the past.

We have also been reminded that faith is a verb—a call to action. James 2:26 tells us, "Faith without works is dead." Our beliefs are not meant to be hidden away but lived out actively, making a tangible impact on the world around us.

Through acts of love, kindness, and service, we demonstrate the transformation God has worked within us, becoming His hands and feet in a world in need of hope and healing.

As we conclude this 40-day journey, let us carry forward the lessons we have learned. Let us embrace the ongoing process of transformation, recognizing that God is continually at work within us. Philippians 1:6 reassures us, "He who began a good work in you will carry it on to completion until the day of Christ Jesus."

May this journey inspire you to live with greater purpose and passion, knowing that you are a beloved child of God, uniquely equipped to make a difference in this world. As you continue to walk in faith, may you experience the profound joy and peace that come from living in alignment with God's divine purpose. Remember, transformation is a journey, not a destination—keep moving forward, trusting in God's promises and His incredible plan for your life.

Acknowledgments

Writing this book has been a journey of faith, discovery, and growth. It would not have been possible without the support and encouragement of many incredible people who have walked alongside me throughout this process. I am deeply grateful to each of you.

First and foremost, I want to thank God for His unending grace, wisdom, and guidance. Without His light in my darkest moments, this book would not have come to fruition. His love and faithfulness have been the foundation of my journey.

To my family, who have been my constant source of strength and inspiration, thank you for your unwavering support and belief in me. Your love has been my anchor, and your encouragement has fueled my passion for writing.

To my wife, Victoria, thank you for your patience, understanding, and endless support. Your love and companionship have been my refuge, and I am blessed to have you by my side.

To Calysta, Zayne, Zion, Erika, and Zealynd, your joy and curiosity remind me daily of the beauty of life and the importance of living with purpose. Thank you for being my inspiration.

A special thank you to my DLC Core Team for your encouragement, feedback, and enthusiasm. Your faith in my work has been invaluable, and I am grateful for your presence in my life.

Finally, to all the readers and supporters who have taken the time to engage with my work, thank you for your interest and encouragement. I hope that this book inspires and grows you in your spiritual journey.

With deepest gratitude,

Manny

About The Author

Manny Rivera, alongside his wife Victoria, has been a transformative leader in ministry for over three decades. Together with their spiritual sons and daughters, they have planted three thriving churches and traveled across the globe, speaking at conferences and training leaders in both ministry and marketplace settings. Manny currently oversees these three churches and serves as the Lead Pastor of Discover Life Church in Lawrenceville, Georgia, where his impact continues to ripple through the lives of his congregation and beyond.

Manny's ministry journey began in an unexpected place—a promising career in baseball. However, a life-altering encounter with Jesus radically changed his trajectory, compelling him to step away from baseball and into full-time ministry. Since then, Manny has been driven by a singular passion: to ignite spiritual revival and raise up the next generation of leaders who will carry the fire of the Gospel.

For over 34 years, Manny has devoted himself to training ministry and business leaders through his Timothy Team, a unique discipleship program designed for those seeking to fulfill God's call on their lives. A relentless pursuit of revival, discipleship, and kingdom advancement fuels his leadership. Known for his raw, unfiltered preaching style, Manny's messages are infused with the power of the Holy Spirit, consistently challenging people to live with conviction, purpose, and a deep connection to Christ.

Manny and Victoria are proud parents to four amazing adult children—Calysta, Zayne, Zion (married to Erika), and Zealynd—who continue to inspire them in their walk with God. Manny finds peace and rejuvenation in nature outside of ministry, often hiking and discovering new trails. His love for travel allows him to engage with diverse cultures and bring the message of Christ to the nations, whether he's speaking at international conferences or building relationships across the world.